'This superb book is written by a historian who has experienced many wars and who has visited Gaza since 1980. Filiu writes, "the Gaza I'd known [had] ceased to exist". The shock and revulsion at what he witnessed there, where death now can come at any time, come through on every page. Written with empathy and deep knowledge of the place and its people, Filiu puts the reader right at the centre of Gaza's horrific reality. I was moved to the bone reading his account, which is like no other I've read on Gaza. Filiu concludes that "this is a world where giving up is disguised as 'realism'". Not so for the author of *A Historian in Gaza*.'
— Raja Shehadeh, Palestinian lawyer, human rights activist and author of *What Does Israel Fear from Palestine?*

'Jean-Pierre Filiu is not just an authority on Gaza, he was there during the genocide. This is not an impassioned screed. *A Historian in Gaza* is a methodical, sober account of Israel's campaign to visit hell upon the people of Gaza and eliminate all aspects of its civil society. An important, essential book.'
— Joe Sacco, cartoonist, journalist, author of *Palestine*, *Footnotes in Gaza*, and *The Once and Future Riot*

'Filiu, the pre-eminent historian of Gaza, tells a factual, and yet passionate, humane story of lives subjected to genocide. In each of the short chapters, Filiu records what happens in homes, families, on the street, in hospitals, in the media and elsewhere, providing a vivid account of unimaginable destruction and ruination while the world watches, and sometimes applauds. This book is an important history of the present of Gaza and its people that should be essential reading to all concerned with humanity and what it means to be human.'
— Dina Matar, Chair of the Centre for Global Media and Communications, SOAS University of London

'Never has the role of historian been more urgent. Filiu's courage, profound insight and first-hand experience make his book a singular contribution to our understanding of the Gaza genocide and its global impact.'
— Mark LeVine, Professor of Modern Middle Eastern History, University of California, Irvine, author of *Impossible Peace: Israel/Palestine since 1989*

'From the viewpoint of its victims, Filiu documents how Israel's extermination machine progressed. He records Gazans' struggle to escape death at the cost of living as traumatised survivors. A must read for those who stay committed to human rights and a better world.'
— Menachem Klein, Professor Emeritus of Political Science, Bar-Ilan University, author of *Lives in Common: Arabs and Jews in Jerusalem, Jaffa and Hebron*

'[A] searing new eyewitness account [and] a much-needed history lesson.'
— *Jacobin*

A HISTORIAN IN GAZA

JEAN-PIERRE FILIU

A Historian in Gaza

Translated by Cynthia Schoch and Trista Selous

HURST & COMPANY, LONDON

First published in the United Kingdom in 2025
By C. Hurst & Co. (Publishers) Ltd.,
New Wing, Somerset House, Strand,
London, WC2R 1LA
All rights reserved.
Originally published as *Un historien à Gaza*, © Les Arènes, Paris, 2025

English-language translation © Cynthia Schoch and Trista Selous, 2025

Printed in Scotland by Bell & Bain Ltd, Glasgow
Distributed in the United States, Canada and Latin America by
Oxford University Press, 198 Madison Avenue, New York, NY 10016,
United States of America.

The right of Jean-Pierre Filiu to be identified as the author of this publication is asserted by him in accordance with the Copyright, Designs and Patents Act, 1988.

A Cataloguing-in-Publication data record for this book is available from the British Library.

ISBN: 9781805265252

EU GPSR Authorised Representative
Easy Access System Europe Oü, 16879218
Address: Mustamäe tee 50, 10621, Tallinn, Estonia
Contact Details: gpsr.requests@easproject.com, +358 40 500 3575

This book is printed using paper from registered sustainable and managed sources.

www.hurstpublishers.com

CONTENTS

Nothing	1
Coordination	7
Shock	17
The Zone	23
The Patriarch	31
One Night	35
Christmas	41
Hospitals	49
Water	61
An Anniversary	73
Witnesses	87
Vultures	101
Death	115
Ingenuity	127
Smoke	139
Waiting	145

Truce	157
One-Fifth	169
Samson	177
Notes	185

NOTHING

NOTHING HAD PREPARED ME for what I saw and experienced in Gaza. Nothing at all. Nothing. Nothing. Not my regular trips to the Palestinian enclave since 1980, not my studies, my research, my fieldwork, not the contacts, friendships, and loyalties formed over the years.

Nothing, not even the works of Gazan artists that have so inspired me, their films, poems, art, or their manifesto against the "nightmare within a nightmare" of Islamist domination under Israeli occupation.

Nothing, especially not the loaded, intense memories of Gaza before the current Catastrophe, fantasised today as a lost paradise but already mutilated by war, by one or other of the fifteen wars Israel has waged against this territory since the Nakba, the Palestinian "Catastrophe" of 1948.

Nothing, despite my conviction, set out countless times, that historically Gaza lies at the heart of Palestine, despite its peripheral location and that, just as any genuine peace with Israel will have to be anchored in Gaza, any conflict launched in Gaza could lead both peoples into an abyss of horror.

Nothing, despite my insistent and repeated appeals for an end to the embargo imposed on Gaza since 2007, while the entire world had grown accustomed to over two million women and men in this besieged "strip" living, at best, excluded from the rest of humanity.

Nothing, despite my ten years of highlighting the "security impasse" facing Israel in basing its security on the total insecurity of Gaza's population, leading it to make not only a moral fault but also a strategic error.

A HISTORIAN IN GAZA

Yet nothing had prepared me for what I saw and experienced in Gaza.

Yes, on 7 October 2023, a few hours after the Hamas terrorist rampage began, I had urged solidarity with all victims, whatever their origin, predicting that this Israeli–Palestinian war would be the most terrible yet in the conflict that had pitted the two peoples against each other for more than a century. At the time, I had also urged the unconditional release of all Israeli hostages, then thought to number around a few dozen, never imagining that there were in fact 251 of them.

Yes, on 22 October 2023, I had already warned Israel and its allies against the risks of a land offensive, urging them "not to fall into the Hamas trap in Gaza",[1] sounding an alarm that would be utterly disregarded five days later, with the beginning of the IDF's (Israeli Defense Forces) reoccupation of Gaza.

Yes, I had subsequently expressed the fear that "behind the stated desire for retaliation lies the desire to eliminate not just Hamas but the Gaza Strip".[2] And I added, "By reducing Gaza to a field of ruins, the Israeli offensive is destroying the very foundations of social and political opposition to Hamas's stranglehold".[3]

Yes, I had taken part in dozens of public events all over France, speaking at universities and secondary schools, city halls and youth centres, bookstores and community cafés, each time repeating that a ceasefire in Gaza was imperative as a precondition for the resolute implementation of the two-state solution, the only prospect of a future for both peoples.

Yes, I had accumulated databases, eyewitness accounts, documents, statistics, field notes, recordings, photographs, and maps to try to gain the most accurate picture possible of the scope and details of the damage inflicted on what had been, until the mid-twentieth century, one of the most prosperous oases in the Middle East.

NOTHING

Yet nothing had prepared me for what I saw and experienced in Gaza.

I had to see and experience it for myself, since fourteen months of gruesome death tolls and alarming analyses had left me with the sense that the reality was slipping away from me, while international organisations were running out of tragic superlatives to describe what they perceived as an unsurpassed horror.

I had to see and experience it for myself, so that my words could once again find meaning in Gaza's reality, while others, far away, wielded words as weapons in a frenzy of competitive self-righteousness, ready to do battle right down to the last Palestinian and the last Israeli.

I had to see and experience it for myself, because Israel has banned foreign journalists from Gaza despite repeated protests and, in Jerusalem, petitions to the Supreme Court, while dozens of Palestinian journalists were being killed in Gaza, sometimes in targeted strikes.

I had to see and experience it for myself, since I'd made two trips to Ukraine in 2023, essential weeks when I could immerse myself in the reality of the war there, even as media outlets the world over were providing remarkable coverage (what would we understand of the war in Ukraine if it was reported only by journalists based in and accredited by Moscow?).

I had to see and experience it for myself, and the only way to do so was to join a humanitarian organisation. Doctors without Borders (Médecins Sans Frontières, MSF) gave me their trust, although responsibility for this book's contents remains solely with me and my publisher.

I had to see and experience it for myself, to retrieve not only the meaning of words in Gaza, but also the simple values of our shared humanity.

Yet nothing had prepared me for what I saw and experienced in Gaza between 19 December 2024 and 21 January 2025.

COORDINATION

NOTHING HAD PREPARED ME to enter the Gaza Strip on foot in the dark of night. Nothing had prepared the IDF soldiers, either, for such an unusual mission—to escort us, some twenty humanitarian workers, through occupied territory, a suitcase in each hand packed with sorely needed supplies rather than personal effects. But our bus, organised by the United Nations with an Israeli police escort, found the gate closed at Kerem Shalom, the "Vineyard of Peace", which is now the only access point to the Gaza Strip for humanitarian workers. After a three-hour wait on the parking lot next to the Egyptian border, the IDF decided to "test" a new approach and accompany our bus northward along the electrified fence that surrounds the Palestinian enclave.

An IDF infantry platoon was waiting for us in front of a breach opened during the invasion of Gaza. Our group of humanitarian workers from all over the world was mustered beneath the stark glare of floodlights. We were told we would be briefed on the next steps of our unprecedented manner of entry into Gaza. But in the end the soldiers didn't speak to us. I soon sensed they were uneasy with the mission they'd been assigned. They were here patrolling this segment of the Gaza Strip to fight Palestinian "terrorists", not escort international humanitarians.

Someone barked an order and the head jeep, headlights blazing, entered Gaza at a crawl. I immediately fell in behind it, my eyes focused on its blinking red lights. It was better not to study the surrounding darkness. Granted, we were now in the buffer zone that Israel had imposed inside the enclave. But we had entered the territory of what was once Rafah, the "citadel of the south", for centuries the gate to Palestine on the edge of Egypt's Sinai desert. This was not how I'd pictured my return to Gaza under siege, on the night of my sixty-third birthday.

The headlights of the jeep bringing up the rear cast our elongated shadows on the dark roadway. The silence was disturbed only by the persistent hum of the engines, the crackling of radios in Hebrew and the sound of our suitcase wheels rolling over military tarmac. Everyone was in a hurry for this to be done with, for the IDF soldiers to hand us over to the UN team, for us to join the armoured vehicles waiting there under unlikely lampposts. For it was only then that we could don the helmets and bulletproof vests that are a must in this war zone.

The "coordination" of our entry into Gaza had promised to go smoothly. For it's important to realise that everything, absolutely everything, must be "coordinated" with the Israeli authorities and receive prior approval before it can enter the Gaza Strip—or indeed leave it. Everyone, Palestinian or foreign; everything, all goods, from humanitarian supplies to commercial items; everything that can be eaten or drunk; everything used to heal or that can be sold; everything, spare parts, pipes and tubing, oxygen tanks and bags of cement, all of them at risk of being turned back on the grounds of a possible "dual use".

Contrary to the dominant perception, this punctilious "coordination" is not the result of the siege Israel imposed on the Gaza Strip after the bloodbath perpetrated by Hamas and its allies on 7 October 2023. Nor does it date from the blockade established in June 2007 against Gaza after Hamas took over. No, it goes back to the Six-Day War in June 1967, when Israel's triumph over the Arab armies gave it control of the Palestinian territory of East Jerusalem, the West Bank and the Gaza Strip,[1] as well as the Sinai Peninsula in Egypt and the Golan Heights in

Syria. Any physical demarcation between Israeli territory and the newly conquered territories was then removed.

The occupation was instituted under the intentionally neutral term "coordination", and overseen by a member of the IDF's General Staff. This "Coordination of Government Activities in the Territories" is referred to by the acronym COGAT. The IDF consolidated its control over Gaza by forcibly displacing one-tenth of the local population and using bulldozers to open military corridors for their tanks. It made use of divisions between the Islamists, who were prepared to collaborate, and the Palestinian nationalists, and capitalised on access to the Israeli market, where cheap labour from Gaza was in high demand. But paradoxically it was a movement towards peace that led to Gaza's increasing enclosure and isolation.

The first Arab–Israeli peace agreement was made between Israel and Egypt, and triggered the phased withdrawal of Israeli forces from Sinai. In 1982 this process ended with the establishment of an international border south of the Palestinian city of Rafah. The occupiers reinforced this border with the Philadelphi Corridor, complete with surveillance patrols and a security fence. In 1994, the Israeli–Palestinian Peace Accords negotiated in Oslo transferred a portion of the West Bank to the control of a "Palestinian Authority" (PA), along with some three-quarters of the Gaza Strip, into which the COGAT continued to "coordinate" entry and exit. The IDF thus offloaded responsibility for directly administering the Palestinian population, focusing instead on protecting the few thousand settlers who had appropriated a quarter of this densely populated territory.

Not only did the Israeli–Palestinian peace agreement fail to reduce the pressure of settlement activity, it also worsened the economic slump in Gaza, where the generosity of international donors did little to offset the loss of income caused by repeated border closures and multiple restrictions. The Erez crossing at the northern entrance to Gaza was growing into an increasingly imposing structure, while the three eastern access points at Nahal Oz, Kissufim and Sufa linked the settlements protected by the army to Israeli territory. Kerem Shalom, more rarely referred to by its Arabic name, Karam Abu Salem, "Abu Salem's Vineyard", controlled the south-eastern tip of the Gaza Strip, where the Philadelphi Corridor ends.

These crossings were all built and managed to ensure Israeli domination over the Gaza Strip, even though international law considers that "the occupying power bears a duty to administer the territory for the benefit of the local population".[2] The use of crossing points as instruments of pressure, even asphyxiation, stems from the refusal to allow the PA to establish an authentic state of Palestine between the West Bank and Gaza, living in peace alongside Israel. Even the withdrawal of the army and settlers from Gaza in September 2005 was carried out without reference to the PA and implemented merely to intensify settlement in the West Bank.

Although the Gaza Strip was evacuated, it remained subject to Israel's arbitrary day-to-day rule. And the sabotage of the two-state solution played into the hands of the Islamists of Hamas, who, after bloody clashes in June 2007, expelled the PA. The Israeli government retaliated by imposing a blockade on Gaza and declaring the entire strip to be "hostile territory".[3] This designation not only assimilates Gaza's entire population to Hamas but also means Israeli citizens who enter the enclave are liable to prosecution.

Since that time, both Gaza's inhabitants and humanitarian organisations have had to put a great deal of energy into "coordination" with the Israeli forces, since only COGAT's green light can offer exemption to a blockade that has become the rule. But in January 2008, the head coordinator also suggested a "model" to the Israeli government, in which some 500 aid trucks would be allowed in every week to prevent malnutrition in Gaza. This calculation was based on the daily requirement of 2,279 calories per inhabitant.[4] The report, intended for internal use only and revealed four years later,[5] speaks volumes about Israel's efforts to manage the existence of Gaza's inhabitants remotely, right down to what was on their plates.

Throughout these sixteen years of blockade, punctuated every two or three years by fighting between Israel and Hamas, I continued to travel regularly to Gaza. The "coordination" of my entrance was usually granted at the last minute, which is why I got into the habit of finding somewhere to stay near a taxi rank in Tel-Aviv so that I could head straight to Erez once I got the green light. There was no time to lose, as the Israeli checkpoint was only open for a few hours a day.

Once my authorisation had been recorded, the formalities were minimal, and always ended with a ritual question: "Are you bringing a weapon into Gaza?" Access was granted once I replied in the negative, while my personal effects vanished on a conveyor belt to be inspected away from my prying eyes.

Once I'd got my luggage back and repacked it—the search was very intrusive—I had to walk several hundred metres along a corridor lined with barbed wire, in the middle of a devastated landscape. This was the buffer zone that Israel had gradually established within Gaza itself. It was not until I had crossed this no man's land that a PA official inspected my passport. I did not have to show it to the Hamas police, despite their strong presence on the other side of the checkpoint. This entirely formal arrangement made it possible to uphold the myth of an "authority" in Gaza recognised by Israel.

On 7 October 2023, Hamas and their allies stormed the Erez crossing, killing and kidnapping the Israeli soldiers and civilians present there. The site the IDF reconquered a few hours later, after heavy fighting, was a scene of devastation. The Gaza Strip was then put under solid siege, which Major General Ghassan Alian, head of COGAT, justified in these terms: "Human animals must be treated as such. There will be no electricity and no water [in Gaza], there will only be destruction. You wanted hell, you will get hell."[6] The head coordinator declared his determination to make the population of Gaza endure "hell", without distinction between civilians and military personnel, irrespective of whether or not they were connected with the now vilified Hamas.

Two weeks after the attack, General Alian announced that "anyone who is within 1000 metres of the security fence is putting his life in danger". With this death threat COGAT formalised the expansion of the buffer zone to a full kilometre inside Gaza, thus depriving the population of some of their most fertile farmland. Soon after that, the IDF began reoccupying Gaza, only loosening its grip to allow a manifestly inadequate flow of aid to trickle in via Egypt. But the Israeli offensive against Rafah in May 2024 closed this access route, while at the same time, in the north of the enclave, the Erez crossing was only briefly reopened, again due to military operations. Kerem Shalom, at Gaza's southern tip, thus became the main bottleneck through which international aid could enter, with lines of trucks waiting for laborious inspection by the IDF. And if there was the slightest doubt about an item in the load, the entire procedure had to be begun again, resulting in delays that could last for weeks. Kerem Shalom was also the only entry point for humanitarian workers in the enclave, providing that they obtained the essential "coordination". It was out of the question for Israel to allow them direct access to Gaza from its own territory. So a tortuous procedure was established, with a route to match, departing from Jordan and prohibiting any kind of stop while in transit through Israel.

The Jerusalem offices of the UN, the International Committee of the Red Cross and humanitarian organizations must request COGAT's green light in order to send aid and personnel. Permission—when it is granted—arrives the evening before a pre-dawn departure from Amman. A Jordanian bus takes you to the Israeli border, then you board an Israeli bus, escorted by the military police, from the River Jordan to Kerem Shalom. Only a few dozen people are admitted into Gaza each week. Medication that is not for personal use is forbidden. Food is limited to three kilos, with a maximum of one kilo per food item.

The trip on 19 December 2024 began promisingly for my group. We crossed the Jordanian border smoothly and most of the "coordinated" were admitted by the Israeli security forces. But then a doctor with an Australian aid organisation, Abdallah Al-Balawi, was interrogated at length and then detained.[7] Three precious hours were lost, a delay compounded by dense traffic around the Jerusalem road junction. Along our route yellow ribbons of solidarity with the hostages detained in Gaza were frequently accompanied by slogans hostile to the prime minister, Benyamin Netanyahu, who was accused of having rejected a prisoner exchange deal with Hamas. When our bus drove up to the Kerem Shalom terminal, the gate was closed and the sun long set.

And so it was that for my birthday the IDF gave me an arrival in Gaza by night and on foot. Nothing could be made out in the surrounding darkness, any vantage point offering a sightline for shooting had been methodically razed. Our group of aid workers did not dally during the ten-minute walk, behind a jeep with headlights blazing, with another bringing up the rear. Our arrival was "coordinated" with a convoy of UN armoured vehicles which we then boarded. Mine bore the number eight and its driver, a sixty-something Filipino, greeted me to the sounds of California surf rock as I slipped on a bulletproof vest and helmet for the occasion.

"Welcome to Gaza!"

SHOCK

R ETURNING TO GAZA AT night in the middle of a war is disturbing enough. But the glimpses of devastation emerging from the shadows as the convoy progresses offer a Dantesque landscape lit up by flashes quickly swallowed by blackness. Ruins heaped in varying states of collapse stream endlessly by, eventually coalescing into a single scene of horror. Here a downed pylon with mangled arms, there a gutted house, further on, a collapsed building.

The convoy advances as fast as the battered road allows. The weather is thankfully decent and our progress is not hindered by mud or potholes. Radios crackle from jeep to jeep with reassuring messages. So far, so good, they echo along the line. We have crossed the invisible frontline, they observe. And soon we'll be out of the zone where looters attack, they inform us, with undisguised relief.

At the north exit from Rafah, the convoy accelerates along Salah al-Din Road—the same Saladin who features in Western tales of the Crusades. It is one of two main roads that traverse the Gaza Strip from north to south. The other is the coast road, once less travelled, but now jammed with waves of displaced Gazans—which is why our guardian angels have opted for Salah al-Din Road. In the distance, occasional pedestrians appear, huddled against the penetrating cold, sometimes alone on the pavement, more often in groups of three or four pulling a makeshift cart. It is unwise to venture out at night in Gaza, where a de facto curfew comes into force as soon as the sun goes down.

A HISTORIAN IN GAZA

The convoy's destination is the former United Nations vocational training centre in Khan Younis, which has become a strategic hub for international aid in the Palestinian enclave due to its central location. It is here that the various agencies come to pick up their personnel. Given the late hour, I am sent to Deir al-Balah and the base camp of the World Health Organization (WHO), which is working directly in Gaza to try to compensate for the destruction of the local health system.

It is nearly midnight when I hear poignant accounts of the tragedy underway in Beit Lahia, in the northernmost part of the enclave, which has been virtually cut off from the world since early October 2024. The term ethnic cleansing does not seem too strong to describe the methodical expulsion of the population, the equally methodical destruction of buildings and the targeting of hospitals, which are the last organised living spaces remaining. I have only just returned to Gaza and already I'm overcome by the tragedy of this besieged territory, through which I passed on my nocturnal journey from Rafah in the south to Deir al-Balah in the centre, to these horrifying descriptions of Beit Lahia.

Next morning the weather is cloudy with intermittent showers as I head back to Khan Younis, this time via the coast road. Tents stretch for kilometres on either side. Some of the displaced have set up makeshift shelters on the beach, braving the gusting winds and breaking waves. Here and there you see a sign announcing a hair salon, a cafeteria or boutique, their names made more enticing by the scarcities within. Drivers have to be careful: pedestrians here are so crushed by pain and traumatised by bombings that they don't always hear vehicles or beeping horns.

Gone is the customary local nonchalance; these are abandoned human beings who come and go, often with the sole aim of waiting for hours for enough water or food to keep them alive for another day. As soon as we start to talk, memories of the many ordeals they've endured come spilling out, dominated by descriptions of their lost home, back there, elsewhere, in the zones of combat and occupation, in the north, the centre, the south, until they found themselves cooped up in what used to be merely an immense wasteland.

They tell me of the dead, the disappeared, the remains still buried under the rubble, of fleeing in panic, gripped by fear, holding children close, being displaced once, twice, ten times, the sorrow and loss, the grief and horror. His eyes fixed on mine, a man with a white beard compares the fate inflicted on the people of Gaza to that of the sacrificial sheep that's fed just enough to have its throat cut during Eid Al-Adha, the most popular celebration on the Muslim calendar.

I'd long understood that the Gaza I'd known and whose length and breadth I'd travelled had ceased to exist. Now this truth has come home to me. And I have a month to try to grasp its poignant reality.

THE ZONE

I WOULD SPEND THIS month inside the "humanitarian zone", as Israel has named a few dozen square kilometres in the centre and south of Gaza. This "zone" primarily comprises the Al-Mawasi coastal strip, along which over a million displaced persons are literally crammed in a sea of tents. Inland it also includes parts of the cities of Deir al-Balah and Khan Younis, the latter far more ravaged than the former. From the south of Al-Mawasi, where I would be staying, I now had an unobstructed view of the shelling, from both land and sea, that was still targeting the last apartment blocks still standing in Rafah, down to the Egyptian border.

"There is no safe place left in the Gaza Strip", as humanitarian organisations have been hammering home for many months, a message that becomes crystal clear in the heart of the besieged enclave. The insistent hum of Israeli drones is only one element in the soundscape of constant attack. Children in Gaza make bets as to who will be first to identify an F-16 fighter jet or Apache helicopter flying over, even if it means bluffing. They're unbeatable when it comes to artillery impacts, machine-gun fire and strikes by the lightweight drones known as quadcopters, which can operate very close to the ground. That these detonations blend with the cock's crow at dawn and the rhythm of the waves makes them no less frightening.

People of all ages have developed a relative notion of distance. When there's a burst of automatic weapons fire, they note without blinking that it's "far off"—a "far off" that can be measured in a few hundred metres, sometimes only two hundred. Or it might be coming from a funeral procession, or, as the local euphemism has it, "family disputes", which tend to be more performative than bloody, despite the very real risk of stray bullets. An Israeli strike, on the other hand, is soon followed by a concert of civil defence sirens, as inhabitants grab their phones to ensure their loved ones have been spared. Information circulates after each dramatic event with astounding speed, images being diffused almost instantly on social media.

Since the start of Israel's blockade in 2007, the Gaza Strip has often been described as "the world's biggest open-air prison". This already densely populated prison lost more of its 365 square kilometres when Israel established a 300-metre buffer zone inside the length of its border. Demonstrators who attempted, in vain, to approach the Israeli fence during the "marches of return" in the spring of 2018 paid the price in dozens of casualties and thousands of wounded. The number of lower limb amputations was unprecedented, even in a Gaza disfigured by cycles of clashes between Hamas and Israel, in 2008–2009, 2012 and 2014.

Yet the men and women of Gaza refer to those years of suffering as the "good old days", literally in Arabic the "sweet days". This is because the Palestinian enclave has been methodically laid to waste since 7 October 2023, with the overwhelming majority of the built environment demolished or damaged. Six days after the start of its offensive, the IDF ordered the departure of more than a million inhabitants from Gaza City and the north of the enclave. Despite this, nearly half the bombardments hit Gaza's supposedly "safe" central zone, which dissuaded some civilians from leaving the north of the Gaza Strip, but prompted a great many others to flee central Gaza toward the south.[1] As for the expansion of the buffer zone along the Israeli border, it sliced off 15 % of the Palestinian enclave's surface area, which had become a no-go zone, on pain of death.

THE ZONE

When on 27 October 2023 the IDF launched its reoccupation of the Gaza Strip, after three weeks of extremely harsh bombardment, nearly 1.5 million inhabitants had already fled their homes. Half of these displaced persons took refuge at United Nations sites, which became saturated at three times their capacity. Over 100,000 civilians crowded into hospitals, churches and public buildings, and a similar number sought shelter in schools. Tens of thousands of others chose to sleep outdoors, but on the edge of a UN site where they believed, mistakenly, that their security would be assured.[2] Due to the destruction of Gaza's last functioning flour mill, people had to wait on average five hours for a ration of bread.[3]

On 1 December 2023, following a seven-day truce—the only pause in fifteen months of hostilities—Israel resurrected fifty-year-old plans for redeveloping the enclave. It divided the Gaza Strip into 620 "blocks", numbered with no coherence whatsoever: Blocks 1 and 2 are adjacent to blocks 20 and 2363, block 50 is next to 219, and the Nuseirat refugee camp is divided into blocks 662 and 2325. It is on the basis of this plan that the population has been displaced in a cascade of evacuation ultimatums, from square to square in a wild game of hopscotch. Residents of one or more blocks receive "advanced warning of an attack" via social media, text message or even airdropped leaflets. Targeted civilians have very little time to make a decision on which their survival and that of their family depends. Flight is not always the safest choice, given the countless examples of inaccurate maps, incoherent data and evacuation routes under fire.[4]

The IDF's methodical destruction has gradually cleared what it calls the Netzarim Corridor, which divides the Palestinian enclave in two.[5] It cuts across the two main north–south roads, Al-Rasheed Road along the coast and Salah al-Din Road, which leads to the Rafah crossing into Egypt. Both these roads, which the invaders describe as "humanitarian corridors", serve to channel the crowds of expelled people towards the south. Palestinian civilians who move from north to south cannot return. And crossing the Israeli roadblocks carries considerable risk, especially for adult males, under threat of arrest, interrogation and even detention, based on facial recognition or random denunciation. Only international aid and humanitarian workers are allowed to travel from south to north in the Gaza Strip.

At the start of 2024, 85 % of Gazans had already been displaced inside the enclave, sometimes several times, due to bombardments. The offensive Israel launched on Rafah on 6 May marked another escalation. The border crossing with Egypt was closed, sealing the Gaza trap around its 2.1 million inhabitants.[6] The IDF captured the some twelve kilometres along the Egyptian border, the Philadelphi Corridor. The crowds of internally displaced persons who had sought some sort of protection from close proximity to Egypt were driven out, this time northward, by fierce fighting in Rafah.

During the summer of 2024, the IDF encroached on territory it had not yet captured, each time using evacuation orders to drive the population further on. On UN maps, the dark pink military zones, with the Netzarim and Philadelphi "corridors" now several kilometres wide, stretch as ruthlessly as the light pink areas, where military operations are covered by evacuation orders. In the zones still white on these maps, humanitarian organisations are required to "notify" their movements to the occupiers, who monitor everything by drone. "Coordination" remains essential for any journey within pink zones, subject to the arbitrary will of the officer on duty.

More than a million people have now been driven to Al-Mawasi, a coastal strip some fifteen kilometres long that Israel defines as a supposedly safe "humanitarian zone". At the start of the twenty-first century, Al-Mawasi was a mere village of about a thousand inhabitants, surrounded by Israeli settlements and off-limits to the rest of the Gazan population. Even Al-Mawasi residents were not allowed to go to the beach down below, which was reserved for settlers. The Israeli withdrawal in 2005 left vast areas unoccupied, forming a "green zone" to which two decades later the invaders decided to push inhabitants of urban centres that were to be "cleansed". In this dumping ground for populations in distress, which could be extended or reduced as hostilities continued, the density exceeds 30,000 people per square kilometre—compared to 1,200 in October 2023.[7] Between May and November 2024, Israel bombed this zone some sixty times, every time claiming to target "terrorists".[8]

Yet it only took Washington's irritation for Israel to consent to loosen its grip. On 13 October 2024, US secretaries of state and defence warned the Israeli government that, failing an improvement in the humanitarian situation in Gaza within thirty days, it would suspend US military aid. Shortly thereafter, the IDF announced the eastward expansion of the "humanitarian zone", enlarging it from 13 % to 19 % of the Gaza Strip. While this extension allowed only a tiny minority of displaced persons to return to largely demolished neighbourhoods in Khan Younis,[9] it was sufficient for US officials to certify that Israel had respected its humanitarian obligations, paving the way for additional arms shipments.

Such certification is yet another scandal in the United States' virtually unconditional support for Israel's war against Gaza. By late 2024, the figures in the UN appraisal of the humanitarian disaster were staggering: 87 % of housing units (411,000) had been destroyed either entirely (141,000), or severely or partially (270,000). Over 80 % of commercial facilities and two-thirds of the road network were damaged.[10] A total of 1.9 million women, men and children had been forced to flee between one and ten times, and a survey of 800 local MSF workers mentioned an average of five consecutive displacements.[11] Nearly a million displaced people were not equipped to face the winter, while half a million were stuck in flood-prone areas. Gaza's displaced had one and a half square metres of space per person in their makeshift shelters. That's right: one and a half square metres.

In the reality behind these data patiently collected by humanitarian organisations there are the open-air rubbish dumps where barefoot children roam. There are the plastic tents that sway in the wind and rain, the semblance of a roof held up by a broom that also serves to sweep out water from repeated leaks. There are the holes dug in the sand for latrines, with tarps strung across to provide a semblance of privacy. There are the domestic wells dug in haste in a corner of the tent, with a basin and a rope to provide for minimal daily needs. There is the stench of stagnant mud that never dries out due to persistent damp. There is the fear of neighbours who are seldom chosen, so close by, so noisy, so invasive. There are the rumours that spread, fuelling resentment and disputes, recriminations and jealousy. There are the endless days with no prospects, spent pining for a ceasefire that's always postponed.

And yet, due to some sort of recurring miracle, all these women and men who have been forced to bend so many times—to enter the family tent, to wash at the bucket, to bear the weight of a few possessions for one, two, three, four, five exoduses, to shield themselves and shield the weakest when the shelling and shooting starts again—these are the very same women and men who, every morning, show themselves to the world as carefully groomed as possible, dignified and upright, courteous and sometimes even smiling, as though emerging from a reality at peace and not the endless nightmare that Gaza has become.

THE PATRIARCH

THE LATIN PATRIARCH OF Jerusalem, Cardinal Pizzaballa, did not have my luck for his own "coordination" to Gaza on 20 December 2024, the day after mine. For eight months this Italian cardinal, the supreme authority of the Catholic church in the Holy Land, had not been able to visit his 500 fellow Christians, who had taken refuge within the Holy Family Church compound in Gaza City. The community was twice this size before this conflict but has now diminished spectacularly due to the flight of 200 Christians to southern Gaza and the departure of 200 more to Egypt (some taking advantage of foreign passports, others paying an Egyptian middleman a tidy sum).

Added to that is the horrific toll of some forty deaths among the Christian community. Half were killed by the IDF: seventeen perished in the airstrike of 19 October 2023 on the Orthodox Church of Saint Porphyrius and, in the following weeks, three women were shot dead inside the Holy Family compound by Israeli snipers. Twenty-one others died due to lack of adequate medical care with pathologies aggravated by malnutrition and lack of drinking water, such as one refugee who succumbed to peritonitis, and another unable to receive his dialysis.[1]

On 20 December 2024, when the Latin Patriarch arrived with his green light from COGAT at Gaza's northern Erez crossing, he was turned away. But Pope Francis was very concerned about the fate of Christians in Gaza, whom he made a point of calling every day.[2] He accused the Israeli authorities of not having kept their "promise", voicing his indignation on this occasion that "Yesterday, children were bombed. It's cruelty. It's not war."³ His remarks, made at a meeting of cardinals at the Vatican, caused such a stir that on 22 December the Israeli government granted the Patriarch permission to visit his flock in Gaza and to spend the night with them, discussing "the end of death and famine", before returning to Bethlehem for the Christmas midnight mass.

The congregation in Gaza's Holy Family Church were deeply moved by Cardinal Pizzaballa's homily with its words of encouragement. "You have become the light of our Church in the entire world", he told them, having explained that "Everyone wanted to come and be with you and bring gifts, but we couldn't carry much"—in reality the Patriarch was accompanied only by an assistant and two nuns, with the baggage restrictions that apply to everyone whose entry into Gaza is "coordinated". He strongly conveyed his community's distress at the endless postponement of any prospect of a ceasefire: "How many promises were made and never fulfilled?"[4] But he was determined to conclude this early Christmas sermon on a note of hope: "Sooner or later, the war will end, and we will rebuild everything: our schools, our hospitals and our homes."[5]

ONE NIGHT

THE NIGHT OF 22 to 23 December 2024, which Cardinal Pizzaballa spent at the Holy Family Church of Gaza, was particularly bloody in the south of the "humanitarian zone". It began with a drone strike on the Fish Fresh tent city, across from the office where I was working. This section of Al-Mawasi gets its name from a once-popular fish restaurant. The seafront is now covered with a mass of tightly packed tents, facing the wind and ocean spray, with only narrow beaten earth paths between them. The strike killed eight people, including two children. A dozen tents caught fire. Panicked survivors tried to put out the fire with the little water they had at their disposal. Armloads of sand were thrown at the spreading flames. The Civil Defence intervened just before the blaze reached a stock of gas canisters. Some twenty injured were evacuated to the nearest hospital.

Then another drone killed two people in a car, not far from where the first missile had hit. Although the two strikes were close in time and place, they were the result of two different war rationales. One was the culmination of a long electronic manhunt targeting a member of Hamas, with no concern for the inevitable "collateral" victims. The other was a deplorable episode in the tug-of-war between Israel and Palestinian Islamists over humanitarian aid. The UN, whose convoys had been regularly looted for weeks, had decided to test a different itinerary. Aid would be conveyed that night via the south of the "humanitarian zone", along the corridor bordering Egypt, and then go up the coast road. Hamas, if only to assert its authority, was determined to handle security for this sixty-six-truck convoy loaded with flour and hygiene kits. But rather than doing the job themselves, the Islamists approached families located along this terribly exposed route.

The IDF, informed of these arrangements, targeted and shot two local notables as they sat in their car, armed and ready to protect the convoy. A few hours later, when looters attacked the aid trucks and met with fierce resistance, Israeli drones came to lend a hand, killing six security guards. The Israeli soldiers also immobilised half the convoy, making it easier for organised attackers to block the road. Some twenty trucks were thus robbed, an impossible stunt to carry out without some form of Israeli complicity from the air. The UN nevertheless considered the loss of one-third of the convoy a relative improvement on the looting of nearly all the previous loads.

Meanwhile at the other end of the enclave, far from international media outlets and humanitarian organisations, another tragedy was unfolding. Kamal Adwan Hospital in Beit Lahia was in its seventy-fifth consecutive day under siege.[1] According to the director, "bombardments didn't stop all night long, nearby houses and buildings have also been destroyed".[2] A few hundred people were trapped inside the medical facility, including about a hundred patients. The inexorable asphyxiation of this hospital had become the symbol of the population drain from the north of the Gaza Strip, where only a few thousand people remained, as opposed to tens of thousands at the start of autumn 2024, and hundreds of thousands one year prior to that.

However, that night was definitely not the worst Gaza had experienced since the beginning of the Israeli offensive. Early in the morning, in Al-Mawasi, I came across the charred remnants of the vehicle gutted by an Israeli drone a few hours before. Then later, in Khan Younis, I saw the funeral procession for the bodies of its two passengers, which had been deposited at the

ONE NIGHT

Nasser hospital morgue during the night and were now being carried along in their white shrouds. Those with them were all men, their faces expressionless, keffiyehs tied tight around their winter jackets, walking in silence. And so it goes with the war and information in Gaza, where tragedies witnessed, even from a distance, combine with the social media echo chamber and its steady flow of first-person accounts and alerts.

CHRISTMAS

DURING THE NIGHT OF 24 to 25 December 2024, the coast of the "humanitarian zone" was whipped by winds. Even if the temperature went no lower than 9° C, it was bitterly cold in the tent that Mahmoud Al-Faseeh had set up directly on the beach. This was a new stage in his wanderings with his family, who had been displaced around ten times in the Gaza City area, before fleeing towards Rafah, then being chased to Al-Mawasi. Mahmoud and his wife Nariman cursed the poverty that prevented them from buying what they needed to protect their children from the wind and cover the damp sand. Their last-born child, Sila, only three weeks old, cried repeatedly during the night. Nariman tried to calm her by holding her close and wrapping her in a blanket.

In the morning, the parents discovered with horror that Sila's body was "like wood", her lips purple and her skin blotchy.[1] Mahmoud rushed her to the nearest hospital, but her lungs were already scarred beyond repair. The director of the children's ward at Nasser Hospital in Khan Younis confirmed her death from hypothermia. It was the hospital's third case of a child who had frozen to death in forty-eight hours; the others were a three-day old newborn and a baby one month old. Staff on the ward said that every day they treated at least five infants with hypothermia, compounded by the inability of exhausted mothers to breastfeed, and by the lack of baby formula due to the blockade.[2] Humanitarian workers had long since run out of blankets and warm clothing and could only recommend parents to warm their infants by holding them skin to skin.

The deaths of these three babies from cold will never be included in the official total of war fatalities. Two names that were recorded, Walaa Frangi and her husband Ahmed Salama, are listed in the Health Ministry's register of deaths with the numbers 45339 and 45340. The couple had been forced to leave their home in Gaza City by an Israeli evacuation order and believed they had found safety south of the Netzarim Corridor, in an apartment block in Nuseirat. It was here that they were killed when the building was bombed, on 25 December 2024.[3] Frangi, a talented calligrapher, had created her own brand of clothing and handcrafts. She enjoyed posing next to her husband, both of them smiling broadly, her head wrapped in a shimmering hijab, his with a cap worn backwards.

Frangi regularly posted photographs of her creations—embroidery, scarves and outfits—on her Instagram account. In May 2024, she posed against the bright blue of the Mediterranean sky as a way of diluting the ruins of Nuseirat. As a soundtrack she had chosen a song by Noel Kharman, a young Palestinian singer-songwriter living in Jordan: "In the soil... we are the roots, we are the foundation, we are the story. This is my place... despite the times." Her last post showed her walking through her devastated neighbourhood, with this comment: "From this gray place, I go out every day trying to find colors and life."[4]

On this same Christmas Day, I go from Al-Mawasi to the city of Khan Younis, at the eastern limit of the "humanitarian zone", inaptly named the "green zone". It's an endless succession of tents, with fences of twisted barbed wire, ill-assorted sheets of corrugated iron and blankets full of holes. A few stunted palm trees, puny fig trees, occasional vegetable plots, and a dozen emaciated camels. Over there, plastic chairs have been brought out of a shelter. Here, an old woman is carried to a ray of sunlight. In another place, a local lad struts around talking on the phone.

CHRISTMAS

Scattered along the roadside are abandoned buses that provide better shelter against the bad weather. One of them displays a yellowed advertisement for the University of Palestine, demolished along with Gaza's eleven other higher education institutions. Further on, next to a pile of old cars, there's a bus sunken in dried mud. Then a café of sorts, where passers-by shoot the breeze around empty tables, beneath faded Real Madrid and Barça banners. Wobbly stalls encroach on the beaten earth of the track. The stream of people walking raises clouds of dust.

Khan Younis takes its name from the Mamluk emir Younis Al-Nawruzi who in 1387 built a caravanserai or *khan* that bore his name and doubled as a staging post. The site was chosen for its abundant water, fertile soil and nearby quarries. The building's central courtyard was reserved for merchants, with lodgings for caravan drivers on the second floor. Protection by a permanent garrison led this commercial crossroads to develop into a major urban centre over the long Ottoman period. Although only one wall of the khan remained during the British mandate, the city continued to spread. After the foundation of Israel in 1948, it was expanded by the addition of a UN-run refugee camp that took in people from all over the lost territory of Palestine.

In December 2023, the IDF launched its first campaign against Khan Younis. Tanks advanced laboriously, supported by airstrikes and heavy shelling. Military bulldozers accompanied their progress, implacably clearing the roads into the city. In April 2024 the Israeli generals withdrew their troops from Khan Younis, leaving the population to dig out hundreds of corpses buried under the rubble. In May the invaders turned the force of their assault on Rafah and the border with Egypt, only to attack Khan Younis with renewed vigour in the last week of July.

The Israeli invasion took Palestinians living in the east of Khan Younis by surprise, forcing them to flee under fire. While Israeli propaganda referred to a mere "adjustment" of the "humanitarian zone", civilians described the violence as "like Doomsday".[5] The Israeli offensive paused for the first week of August 2024 before going on again until the end of the month. The relentless battle against Khan Younis had the stated objective of "degrading" the military capabilities of Hamas and eliminating Yahya Sinwar, a native of the city and mastermind of the 7 October 2023 attack. However, Sinwar was ultimately killed during a routine patrol in Rafah, well south of Khan Younis, on 17 October 2024.

I enter Khan Younis between the Jordanian field hospital and a cemetery open to the winds, and come across some employees of the Khan Younis Municipality—yet another civilian institution that has been destroyed. They now work for the International Red Cross dispatching piles of waste with rudimentary tools. A canvas hut between two collapsed buildings serves as a pharmacy. The sandy road is deeply rutted, but a benevolent ray of sunlight guides us through without getting bogged down. One last bend and there before me in a panorama lies what was once Khan Younis.

And there, overwhelmed, I make my way in search of landmarks that have been reduced to dust, teetering between gaping craters and piles of rubble. Although I have been in a number of war zones in the past, from Ukraine to Afghanistan, Syria, Iraq and Somalia, never, ever, have I experienced anything of the like. I had read descriptions comparing it to a "moonscape" or a "scene of apocalypse", I'd heard competitive clashes between ever more extreme superlatives, I'd examined before and after satellite images. Now I have a better understanding of why Israel has denied the international media access to such an appalling scene.

I prefer to cling to the shards of life surfacing from the wreckage. Little girls with school bags on their backs emerge from the far end of an alleyway, where they attend classes provided by an institution supported by the Sultanate of Oman. A survivor who has erected his tent amid the rubble maintains a decent interior by emptying a bucket of refuse outside his "door". A family has found refuge on the top floor of a disfigured building and are drying their laundry on a rickety balcony. Tents provide patches of colour—green, blue, red—in an ash-grey world. Crooked stalls display canned goods, two or three trinkets and a few sweets.

Here and there, if you dare to scrutinise the rubble, life can be seen discreetly, stubbornly, creeping out. And the devastation is never uniform. Near the centre of Khan Younis, some apartment blocks have come through the Russian roulette of shelling hardly burnt at all, and the traditional meeting hall of a local clan has been completely spared. The Sheikh Nasser intersection strikes a singular note, with its animated tangle of motorcycles, carts and tuk-tuks. But just head north and it's a new litany of ruins. A mosque has been reduced to no more than a pockmarked minaret. An entire street is blocked by a collapsed building. On either side of Salah al-Din Road, there's nothing of the urban fabric left to see. And even if Dar Essalam Hospital, the "House of Peace", still stands tall, it's just an empty shell, charred and ravaged on the inside.

Here lies the city of Khan Younis on this Christmas Day.

HOSPITALS

EARLY IN THE MORNING of 27 December 2024, in Beit Lahia, in the north of the Gaza Strip, the IDF gave a fifteen-minute warning to evacuate Kamal Adwan Hospital. All of Gaza followed the news of its occupants—around 350 including 75 sick and wounded—in real time. For eighty days, the attackers had been tightening their grip on the hospital, from which ever more desperate calls for help could be heard. Despite repeated requests from the United Nations, the last convoy of aid dated back to 20 December and a delivery of 5,000 litres of fuel and 100 units of blood.[1] But these relief supplies provided little respite—just enough to keep the intensive care ward operational. The Israeli strikes were coming closer and closer, initially carried out by drones and, in the final phase, by remote-controlled vehicles loaded with explosives. On 26 December five of the hospital staff were killed, including a paediatrician and two ambulance drivers.[2]

Hussam Abu Safiya, the hospital director, epitomised the determination of an ever-diminishing number of inhabitants in northern Gaza to cling to their land. On 6 October 2024 the IDF had begun a new phase of its war, this time aiming to completely destroy the area north of Gaza City and empty it of its population. Abu Safiya refused the order to evacuate the hospital, declaring that no combatants were hiding there.[3] On 25 October Israeli fire injured three of the staff and destroyed medical supplies that the WHO had recently delivered. The attack also damaged the medical oxygen generator, resulting in the death of two newborns.[4] Soldiers then burst into the hospital and detained staff and patients for questioning. In this raid, one of the director's sons was killed by a drone strike at the hospital entrance. Overcome with grief, the next day Abu Safiya nevertheless found the strength to lead a prayer for his son and bury him by one of the walls.

The IDF withdrew from the hospital compound on 28 October 2024, but resumed shelling three days later, again destroying a shipment of supplies from the WHO. Between 3 and 5 November, the paediatric ward and water tanks were damaged by strikes. On 23 November, Abu Safiya was wounded in the leg by a piece of shrapnel. He considered it an "honour" to have been hit at his workplace and soon returned to providing care. He was one of only two doctors still working at the hospital and complained of being "forced to choose between patients due to the overwhelming numbers of wounded". All his ambulances were out of service and hostilities in Beit Lahia continued unabated.[5] The attacks increased in intensity, with the forced evacuation of more than 2,000 civilians on 14 December, and culminated in a final assault on 27 December.

Israeli soldiers used loudspeakers to order patients and staff to leave the hospital. They then stormed the building, setting several fires and alarming the WHO.[6] With no running water to douse the flames, panicking staff tried to put them out with dialysis liquid, which contains inflammable and corrosive substances. Some individuals were seriously burned and one patient died in the fire.[7] The surgical unit, operating theatre, central pharmacy and laboratory were seriously damaged.[8]

Videos by Israeli soldiers show them seizing medical files, binders and a wide range of documents from the archives before setting fire to the premises. Fifteen patients in critical condition, fifty nursing staff and twenty healthcare workers were taken south to Jabaliya, half-way to Gaza City, and left at the Indonesian

Hospital there, even though this hospital had itself been stormed three days earlier and was no longer functioning. The new arrivals were left shivering in a building with no window panes and no running water, using curtains as blankets for patients.[9]

The remaining evacuees from Kamal Adwan Hospital were forced to walk to an Israeli roadblock, where men and women were separated and their phones confiscated. During the long wait that followed, they were each subjected to an extensive search. Women who refused by gripping their clothing were roughly manhandled and insulted until they complied.[10] As for the men, soldiers made them strip down to their underwear, jeering and harshly beating those who refused, including an injured man in a plaster cast.[11] Some were then made to walk in single file between two Israeli armoured vehicles that trained their guns on them.[12] Others, semi-naked in the cold, were subjected to the humiliation of having a number written in felt marker on their necks or their chests.[13] Then all were lined up between two jeeps, one in front, the other behind, and forced to make the exhausting march to northern Gaza, where they were left to their own devices.

The attackers took Abu Safiya and some twenty other civilians from Kamal Adwan Hospital and transferred them to an unknown destination. Israeli propaganda accused the director of being "a Hamas operative".[14] A photograph that quickly went viral shows him alone, from the back, in his white coat, walking towards two tanks stationed in the middle of the ruins. This is the last image of him at liberty. Palestinians detained in the Sde Teiman military prison in the Israeli Negev desert said that Abu Safiya was being held there and had been severely beaten. Concern for his safety was all the more serious given that systematic ill treatment at Sde Teiman has been documented for months.[15] Indeed, revelations in the Israeli media about the sexual abuse of prisoners at Sde Teiman sparked clashes between the police and ultranationalists, who had come to protest the arrest of nine reservists suspected of having raped a Palestinian detainee.[16]

On 29 December 2024, the top floors of two hospitals in Gaza City, Al-Wafaa, although out of service and undergoing rehabilitation, and Al-Ahli, known as Baptist,[17] were bombed, with seven killed at Al-Wafaa. The following day, the WHO organised the evacuation of ten patients in a critical condition to the Indonesian Hospital. But some twenty Israeli soldiers intercepted the convoy and took four of the patients, including a hemiplegic, and threw them into an armoured vehicle. The abduction led the WHO director general to make a formal complaint, and to insist that Israel guarantee the prisoners' medical needs and their rights. He called for the "immediate release" of Abu Safiya, lamenting that "hospitals in Gaza had once again become battlegrounds".[18]

The demise of Kamal Adwan Hospital was only the latest episode in a series of attacks by the IDF against medical facilities in Gaza. Netanyahu and his government have regularly justified these violations of humanitarian law by claiming that Hamas had turned these compounds into "terrorist strongholds".[19] However, they have yet to provide irrefutable proof of these serious allegations.[20] On the other hand it was documented that the IDF used the medical facilities it occupied to conduct its own military operations.[21] Israel's propaganda manipulations have finally managed to shock media outlets that remain critical of the parallel propaganda put out by Hamas.[22]

One example features the IDF spokesperson at the Al-Rantisi paediatric hospital in northern Gaza City, on 13 November 2023, three days after the staff and patients had been forced to evacuate, waving scraps of white cloth. The general poses in a basement room of the hospital, holding up a length of rope tied to a chair, which he claims as proof that hostages were being held there. He then holds up a baby's bottle as evidence that children were present. Then he waves a piece of paper at the camera, claiming it is a list of jailers on which each terrorist is assigned his turn to stand guard. This supposed documentary evidence turned out to be a calendar in Arabic with an Islamist slogan added in pen.[23] As for the underground room, hospital staff countered that it was a shelter for civilians in the event of bombardment, which explained the presence of a toilet and curtains for privacy.

Another propaganda operation targeting the Al-Shifa Hospital in central Gaza City was done with more professionalism. The IDF asserted "with certainty", using 3D imagery, that there was an underground "command centre" on three interconnected levels below the emergency department. The 600-bed Al-Shifa was Gaza's largest hospital and provided shelter for more than 2,000 people, at least half of them civilians, until it was forcibly evacuated on 19 November 2023.[24] Yet the videos broadcast by the Israeli military after its takeover of the hospital show nothing more than a tunnel a good one hundred metres long, with two exits at some distance from the emergency department. The weapons supposedly found within the hospital had in fact been seized from vehicles parked outside.[25] Comparison of two recordings of the "discovery" of a bag of guns behind an MRI machine revealed that the number of weapons had doubled from one video to the next.[26]

The Geneva Convention IV, adopted in 1949, which sets out the international humanitarian law in this domain, unambiguously states that "civilian hospitals organized to give care to the wounded and sick, the infirm and maternity cases, may in no circumstances be the object of attack". This protection may be suspended if the hospital is used to commit "acts harmful to the enemy", but only after "due warning" has been given. Moreover, "the fact that sick or wounded members of the armed forces are nursed in these hospitals, or the presence of small arms and ammunition taken from such combatants and not yet handed to the proper service, shall not be considered to be acts harmful to the enemy".[27]

Even when the IDF has not accused a hospital of harbouring Hamas combatants, that does not mean it will be spared. An example is the Al-Awda Hospital in Jabaliya, northern Gaza, which was encircled by IDF troops in autumn 2023. On 21 November, artillery fire killed four people there, including three doctors, and injured three, including two nurses. The third and fourth floors of the building suffered considerable damage. On 7 December, a nurse was shot in the chest and died. A hospital staff member was shot in the head on 9 December, and another on 21 December. And on 6 and 8 December, in separate incidents, two pregnant women were killed some twenty metres from the hospital entrance while trying to reach it to give birth.[28]

Nasser Hospital, in the west of Khan Younis, bore the full force of the invasion of the city that began on 1 December 2023. Thousands of people sought refuge there, though some were also seeking care. The maternity ward was hit on 17 December, killing a teenage girl. IDF troops cordoned off the perimeter of the hospital on 21 January 2024, which made it impossible to evacuate the area when the order to do so was issued two days later. Eight hundred and fifty patients and thousands of refugees were trapped in the hospital compound, which faced a cruel shortage of medical supplies. Abdominal gauze was reused again and again. The blood would be squeezed out and the gauze washed and sterilised for the next patient.[29] No one knew if it was more dangerous to stay in the hospital or flee while the hostilities continued.

On 13 February 2024 the attackers withdrew permission for anyone to remain, beyond the healthcare staff, patients, and one care-giver per patient. All other refugees were ordered to leave. Panic spread when an Israeli strike killed three people inside the hospital and injured ten more. The following night a shell killed one person and injured ten. At dawn on 15 February, Israeli soldiers stormed the hospital and destroyed equipment and ambulances, before systematically screening everyone inside. They drew an x on the knee of those they planned to interrogate on site and an x on the forehead of those they would take to an unknown destination.[30] The following day, the electricity was cut off, resulting in the death of four patients in intensive care. The next day, water and food ran out. Yet it wasn't until 22 February that the IDF evacuated this badly damaged hospital that was no longer operational, that had no water, food or electricity, but where around a hundred patients still remained.

Israel's endless war against Gaza, rather than Hamas, unfolds in an exhausting series of sieges, occupations and evacuations of its various hospitals. Some have managed to overcome the shock of this violence and resume operations, repairing and rehabilitating their facilities in order to go on serving their community. Others, devastated by the hostilities, were forced to close after the first or second attack. During the first ten months of the conflict alone, 35 of Gaza's 36 hospitals were put out of service at least once, 31 were hit by Israeli strikes, 11 were placed under siege (5 of them twice) and 10 were occupied (4 of them twice).[31]

Yet the IDF is perfectly capable of sparing a hospital in a combat zone when it wants to. The case of the field hospital opened in Rafah by the United Arab Emirates, in December 2023, proves this beyond a doubt. The Emirates were signatories to the only strategic partnership treaty between Israel and an Arab state, as part of the Abraham Accords. The ambition of this treaty contrasts with the half-hearted peace agreements signed by Egypt and by Jordan. The Emirati hospital was built in Rafah, for its proximity with what was then the open border with Egypt, in an area still spared at that time by the hostilities raging in the north. It is the flagship of operation "Gallant Knight", launched by Abu Dhabi to enable it to spearhead "humanitarian activism" in Gaza.

The Israeli offensive on Rafah launched in May 2024 did no damage whatsoever to the Emirati hospital, even as the population deserted the city and evacuation orders were issued in quick succession. Although bombing intensified and buildings collapsed all around it, the medical centre's state-of-the-art facilities and hundred or so beds remained as pristine as the day it opened. True, the Indian maintenance staff were hired in Abu Dhabi, as were the expatriate doctors. Increasingly cut off from its local environment, the Emirati hospital was reduced to conducting consultations via Starlink, while boasting that it offered "the highest level of medical care for Palestinian patients".[32] It was well and truly a "humanitarian bubble", the main function of which had become simply to draw up the assistance protocols for medical evacuations to the United Arab Emirates.[33]

Meanwhile, Israel's assaults on Gaza's other hospitals were having a devastating impact well beyond the hospital walls. The congestion seen in emergency departments during the bloodiest battles forced surgeons to make drastic choices in prioritising operations. According to the UN, "Many injured reportedly died while waiting to be hospitalized or treated".[34] Even those who did receive surgery were often discharged prematurely due to lack of space. Care for the wounded was seriously jeopardised by the lack of bandages, shortages of drugs and medicine and repeated expulsions. In addition, the thousand or so patients requiring regular dialysis and some 10,000 cancer patients lost vital access to treatment and monitoring.[35] Again according to the UN, "a number of newborns died because their mothers were unable to attend postnatal check-ups or reach medical facilities to give birth".[36]

HOSPITALS

It's important to note Israel's obstructive approach to the entry of medical equipment and anaesthetics into Gaza, and its hospital sieges that deprive them of essential supplies. The warrants issued by the International Criminal Court on 21 November 2024 for Netanyahu and his Minister of Defense, Yoav Gallant, accuse them of a specific "crime against humanity": "by intentionally limiting or preventing medical supplies and medicine from getting into Gaza", they are deemed "responsible for inflicting great suffering by means of inhumane acts on persons in need of treatment", because doctors have been "forced to operate on wounded persons and carry out amputations, including on children, without anaesthetics".[37]

The health system that has suffered an ordeal by fire since October 2023 was robust and diverse. Its primary resource was a medical corps—doctors, nurses and ambulance drivers—with prior exposure to wartime emergencies. This unique experience enabled them not to fall apart as soon as the IDF onslaught began. And the countless testimonies to their discreet devotion, proven courage, and even pure heroism command respect. Healthcare staff may learn while on duty that an evacuation order has been issued in the block where their families live. Rather than return to be with their loved ones, they often decide to remain at work to fulfil their mission.

The price of such selflessness is mind-boggling. One year into the conflict, at least 587 of them have been killed, including 185 nurses, 91 doctors, 57 ambulance drivers, 51 pharmacists, 42 physiotherapists and as many dentists.[38] More healthcare workers have been killed in Gaza since October 2023 than in all conflicts globally in 2021 and 2022 combined.[39] MSF has already lost twelve of its staff. Israeli artillery fire on Al-Awda Hospital on 21 November 2023 killed two of its doctors, Ahmad Al-Sahar and Mahmoud Abu Nujeila. Shortly before dying, Abu Nujeila wrote on the whiteboard normally used for planning surgeries "Whoever stays until the end will tell the story. We did what we could. Remember us."[40]

"We did what we could."

"Remember us."

WATER

IN THE SMALL HOURS of 30 December 2024, Gaza was struck by a heavy downpour that hit the "humanitarian zone" with full force. The fact that the ten previous days had been fairly sunny made its impact all the more dreadful. Before this war, Gazans used to greet the rain with joy as it brought life to the now vanished fields and orchards. There were even specific prayers to bring the rain down from the sky and to express gratitude when it came. All of that, like all the rest, is well and truly in the past. Rain is merely another enemy to be neutralised in the daily battle for survival. Once again, people have to hold on, literally, so as not to drown. An old man tries to keep his spirits up by telling his neighbours, "The rain lightens our mood."

At daybreak, people check on each others' situations after a sleepless night. In the back of carts, in the queue for flour, at a busy intersection, they ask who managed to shield their children from this latest ordeal, who had their tent collapse on their head, whose meagre possessions were mercilessly drenched. Those who were relatively spared give thanks to God for their luck. Those who spent hours bailing out muddy water and cursing the collapse of their plastic roof merely mention that the night has been "difficult". But those who shovelled out the muck and were still shovelling as the tide rose, hollow of eye, shallow of breath, hoping to spare their freezing children the worst, they say nothing.

The hand-dug wells that dot the sandy shoreline threaten to overflow with each storm. The powerless population is sometimes caught between groundwater overflows and torrential rains, while puddles coalesce into ever more treacherous pools. After a welcome respite in the daylight hours of 30 December, the weather turned from bad to worse during the night. The most exposed refugees are those who set up their tents at the sea's edge. They had ended up on the beach because there was less competition for space, and gradually encroached on the coast road. The following day, gusts of wind hit them with full force, flooding and destroying hundreds of tents. Mid-morning, a burst of automatic gunfire from the Israeli navy nearby caused conversations to fall silent for a moment. But it was soon muffled by crashing thunder and pounding hail.

Water cascades down for hours and torrential streams of mud flow between the tents. To ward off calamity, the refugees band together in the driving rain and dig hasty, inadequate trenches around their shelters. Shovels pass from hand to hand, feet sink into the muck and encouragement is found in memories of better days. The earth removed is piled into makeshift dikes and canvas sacks long since empty of flour to bolster the perimeter of the camp. It's a battle on every front to mend the fabric of the tents, patch the many leaks and repair the poles that hold up these fragile dwellings.

The men keep their fatigue and suffering to themselves, but a dignified old woman, shivering in a threadbare shawl, cries out to the heavens that she has "never been so cold or so hungry".[1] Another woman, soaked to the bone, weeps over her drenched mattresses and declares herself willing to go without food: "It's not food that we want, we just want to be dry. We want a dry place to sit, we just want a bit of warmth. Warmth!"[2] A tearful woman sloshing around in her tent laments that her family "fled fire only to end up drowned".[3] Clotheslines swing in the rain hung with garments left out, because here, as everywhere else, everything is soaked. Grave-faced kids make themselves busy, one sponging up the mud and scraping it with a brush, another scooping up puddle after puddle into a bucket, a third pushing a wheelbarrow full of earth.

While water from the sky blindly wreaks its havoc, drinking water still has to be collected for daily consumption. Refugees mill around water distribution points with 5, 10 and 25-litre jerrycans in transparent, yellow or blue plastic. Some are marked with a number, or even a surname, ready to be placed in the line that forms well before opening time. It's best to arrive early, when the water pressure is at its strongest. Some bring open basins, metal tins—all manner of receptacles, even if it means spilling some of the precious liquid as onlookers make sarcastic remarks. The tacit limit is fifty litres per extended family, a load that is carried by two grunting adults. A little girl pulls a cart behind which a group of kids each drag a jerrycan half their size.

Such desolation obscures the fact that for thousands of years Gaza was an oasis known for its rich vegetation and gentle climate. The Wadi Gaza, a river that meets the Mediterranean south of Gaza City, once had a much greater flow rate than the famous River Jordan. It nourished the largest wetland in all of historic Palestine, known for its orchards and its palm groves. Gaza's prosperity relied largely on exports of grain and citrus fruit, the former dominating in the late Ottoman period, until citrus took over during the British mandate and under Egyptian rule.

The 1967 occupation is when Gaza's water resources came under Israeli control, first with the installation of Mekorot, Israel's national water utility, and then diversion to the settlements. Although the settlers themselves, a mostly radical group, numbered no more than a few thousand, they appropriated a quarter of Gaza's land and received a disproportionate allocation of water. The scorched earth policy that characterised Israel's unilateral withdrawal in 2005 meant Gazans could make no use of the infrastructure established for the benefit of the settlers. The IDF made sure to keep the entire territory under its close control, a grip that tightened in 2007 after Hamas took power and the strict blockade was implemented.

Israeli control, henceforth from a distance, aggravated a vicious circle that saw demographic pressure lead to the excessive extraction of groundwater, itself increasingly infiltrated by sea water, which is now increasingly contaminated by discharges of wastewater into the Mediterranean. In 2021, only 7 % of the water consumed in the Gaza Strip was supplied by three desalination plants, which also chlorinate seawater, while 13 % was delivered by Mekorot pipelines.[4] To enjoy Israeli water quality one had to be connected to this network, pay a surcharge and be able to store reserves, as the water flow is intermittent.

The remaining 80 % of Gazan water was drawn from some three hundred public and private wells drilled into the aquifer. This water is unfit for human consumption unless it is desalinated and purified. Prior to the start of the current conflict, the daily amount of water available per person in the Gaza Strip was approximately 80 litres—three times less than in Israel. In the final days of 2024 it fell to nine litres per person per day, of which only two litres were fit to drink.[5] This average figure masks grave disparities in access to a vital resource that has now become so scarce.

The deterioration in water supply is the result of a deliberate policy conducted by Netanyahu and his government. The siege imposed in retaliation for the Hamas attacks on 7 October 2023 brought Gaza to a halt, with the complete cessation of deliveries of electricity, fuel and water. Fuel deliveries resumed a month later, but at a rate that, according to the UN, covers only about one-fifth of the needs of "the most basic humanitarian operations".[6] These brutal restrictions hinder the running of desalination plants and wells, which have become largely dependent on their backup generators. The use of solar panels is now only marginal and limited to the small scale, as the IDF has destroyed the large solar power plants.

Mekorot resumed water delivery in November 2023, a few days after the land invasion of Gaza. But the central pipeline was the only one functioning. The northern pipeline had been breached by Israeli bombardment and the one in the south sustained critical damage shortly afterwards. A substitute pipeline running from Egypt, provided by the United Arab Emirates in February 2024, was rendered non-functional three months later by the Israeli offensive on Rafah. Mekorot gradually reopened its three pipelines, though at no more than three-quarters of their former flow.[7] In any case, the massive and repeated population displacements prevented most people from accessing the Israeli network. In conversations in Gaza, people talk nostalgically about the incomparable taste of water from Mekorot, "sweet as honey".

Fuel shortages meant that the three desalination plants were functioning at only 10 % capacity in January 2024, and at 15 % three months later.[8] The shortages also put at least half of Gaza's wells out of service. And even those wells that were still operable encountered huge difficulties in carrying out desalination and purification. Refugees have had to decide between water drawn from close to the surface but unfit for consumption, and water from deeper underground, but saline due to seawater infiltration. Unscrupulous entrepreneurs resort to the first option for their on-demand deliveries. To add to all this, septic tanks in the encampments are dug in haste and tend to overflow at the slightest storm, threatening to contaminate nearby wells. At the humble personal level, and for the first time in my life, I have indulged in the luxury of brushing my teeth solely with drinking water.

A HISTORIAN IN GAZA

The chaotic situation has made it impossible for international organisations to carry out the systematic inspection of the quality of the water available at scheduled distribution points and from tanker trucks. The roads through the "humanitarian zone", already overrun by makeshift stalls and the tents of the displaced, offer the spectacle of vehicles of all kinds transporting at least one—usually black—tank containing a cubic metre of water. Pick-up trucks, donkey carts and tractors cross Gaza in all directions, periodically blocking the traffic as they deliver to a building or community. It's advisable to remain patient while they unroll their hoses and work their way through a queue of customers with jerrycans at their feet.

By late January 2024, the UN estimated that 87 % of the sanitation infrastructure in Gaza City had been destroyed or damaged, 82 % in northern Gaza, 54 % in Deir al-Balah and 46 % in Khan Younis.[9] The IDF had been given the GPS coordinates of the plants, arousing suspicions that the strikes were deliberate. When military bulldozers demolished the solar farms powering four of Gaza's six wastewater treatment plants, the intent to inflict damage was clear.[10] A pattern seems to repeat itself, in which the Israeli authorities agree to make minor gestures towards water provision, while demolishing sanitation plants and killing their workers without compunction.[11]

The impact of these strikes was compounded by impediments to getting essential water treatment products and equipment into Gaza. It wasn't until six months into the conflict that the public water treatment facility received its first deliveries of chlorine. Provision remained erratic in Gaza City and the north of the enclave, stabilizing only in September 2024.[12] The IDF has a very rigid conception of civilian and military "dual use" that does not comply with internationally approved criteria.[13] The presence of a single "suspect" item results in the truck being turned away and an additional twenty-day wait. Items sometimes denied access include desalination equipment, flexible tanks, water quality testing kits, spare parts and even portable latrines.

The combination of water pollution and obstacles to treating this already scarce resource has led to a disastrous spread of infectious diseases. By January 2024, UNICEF had recorded 71,000 cases of diarrhoea weekly among children under five—one in four children—as opposed to 2,000 cases prior to the start of the conflict.[14] Dehydration has caused a spectacular rise in urinary tract infections (UTIs) and kidney complaints in the population at large. Women are particularly vulnerable due to the constraints of life in densely packed tents. As of October 2024, 669,000 cases of acute diarrhoea had been recorded in one year of hostilities, with one in three inhabitants affected. Added to that were 132,000 cases of severe jaundice, a very concerning indicator of the prevalence of hepatitis A.[15] Skin diseases, particularly scabies, are spreading dangerously, aggravated by the high water salinity.

Calamitous sanitary conditions are aggravated by shortages of detergent and soap. A 75-gramme bar of soap cost the equivalent of at least $10 in Gazan markets in late summer 2024.[16] Palestinian family budgets, already strained due to repeated displacements, have been further stretched by the prohibitive cost of everyday hygiene products, added to the expense of drinking water from private suppliers. The use of caustic soda as a household detergent has been the cause of several accidents in the tents, usually affecting children. As the different statistics show, the list of scourges visited upon the population of Gaza is absolutely staggering.

Polio had disappeared from the Gaza Strip for a quarter century and was supposed to be definitively eradicated. But on 17 August 2024, the first case of polio was confirmed in Deir al-Balah in a ten-month-old child. The IDF, concerned that traces of the virus had been found in wastewater samples in Gaza, had already decided weeks before to vaccinate all its troops on active duty. The spread of polio has been facilitated by the accumulation of 340,000 tons of solid waste across Gaza, representing a thousand tons per square kilometre, and an even higher density in the so-called "green zone".[17] The risk of contagion coupled with the international outcry forced Israel to agree to "humanitarian pauses" so that a widespread vaccination campaign could be conducted.

Netanyahu only agreed to this in exchange for new concessions on the ground. On 30 August 2024, after bitter debate, his government undertook to maintain Israeli troops in the Philadelphi Corridor along the Egyptian border, which had already been occupied for nearly four months. Former General Yoav Gallant, the Minister of Defence, unsuccessfully opposed this decision, on the grounds that "clean-up operations" in the zone had achieved their military objectives. The United States, which had warned, also in vain, against the humanitarian risks of an offensive on Rafah, simply acknowledged the Israeli prime minister's latest power play. Netanyahu used the occasion to tout the "humanitarian" generosity of the vaccination campaign in Gaza.

The campaign began on 31 August 2024. Two drops of vaccine were administered to children orally, with a second dose required between four and six weeks later. The IDF allowed UN refrigerator trucks carrying a double dose of vaccines for all children under 10 to enter Gaza. It also decreed "humanitarian pauses" from 8 am to 3 pm on three or even four days in the areas opened for vaccination, first in central and southern Gaza, then in the north. The campaign was carried out by a thousand or so Palestinian health workers. On 9 September it seemed at risk when a UN convoy, which had of course been "coordinated", was damaged by Israeli bulldozers.[18] The operation was nevertheless completed, with at least 90 % of the eligible population being vaccinated.[19]

WATER

The offensive the IDF launched in northern Gaza on 6 October 2024 jeopardised the second phase of the vaccination campaign. The campaign in central and southern Gaza was successful, with 450,000 children receiving their second dose of vaccine, along with a vitamin A supplement. But the UN decided to postpone the vaccination measures in the north "due to the escalating violence, intense bombardment, mass displacement orders, and lack of assured humanitarian pauses".[20] The aim was to replicate the approach of the first phase, conducting vaccinations both in Gaza City and to the north, in Jabaliya, Beit Lahia and Beit Hanoun.

Despite US diplomatic efforts, the IDF refused to grant vaccination teams access to the zone where it was expelling the population. The United Nations finally gave in to avoid losing the benefit of the campaign's first phase, since the deadline for administering the second dose was fast approaching. It agreed to exclude approximately 15,000 children from the second phase, and to pursue the campaign despite an attack that injured six people, four of them children, in a vaccination centre in Gaza City.[21] Most likely due to this incomplete vaccination programme, traces of the polio virus were again detected in December, requiring the scheduling of another campaign in 2025. The immunisation coverage of children in Gaza, which had been practically universal for diphtheria, tetanus, measles and whooping cough, is now at less than 90 %, with the ensuing risk of epidemic outbreaks.

Twenty percent of the water sampled by specialised agencies across Gaza in December 2024 turned up the presence of faecal matter. Seventy-three percent of the water considered drinkable and 97 % of water for domestic use did not meet international standards for purity due to a lack of systematic chlorination. All in all, the local water production amounted to less than a quarter of the pre-October 2023 level. And this remaining quantity was further reduced by 70 % due to leaks in the distribution network and the limited number of tankers, which could not be offset by carts with their tanks holding one cubic metre.[22] As always in Gaza, dry statistics, however shocking, cannot truly convey the scale of the disaster.

At this point, I might mention the little girl avidly sucking on a pipe sticking out of a desalination plant. Describe the fatigue and despondency of queues at water points. Mention the mothers sitting in the sand in front of their tents, stirring an almost empty pan for the family meal. Once over the shock I'd had at Christmas, I went back to the ruins of central Khan Younis. Here, in the midst of piles of rubble that were once houses, shops and schools, I see a tree, bent over and covered in dust, stuck beneath a balcony hanging in the void—and then another tree, rising up with more confidence. And I feel a fragile strand of life: people crossing paths and greeting one another, more market stalls and children less dazed than elsewhere.

I ask around and they show me, way up there above a huge pile of rubble, a water tower standing as an unlikely sentinel. Yes, a water tower that by some mysterious chance has survived bombings and military sweeps. Its water quality is dubious, but it keeps this devastated community on their feet. Yes, it's true, in the flourishing oasis that was Gaza for thousands of years, an oasis dreamed of by caravan drivers and celebrated by chroniclers, an oasis since cut off from the world and reduced to a "strip" of land, yes, in this oasis of despair that is the Gaza Strip under siege, vegetation still manages to spring back to life amid the ruins.

AN ANNIVERSARY

T HE SUNSHINE THAT USHERED in 2025 facilitated laborious repairs to the damage done the day before. From one tent to the next, people set to work and thanked God they'd overcome yet another ordeal. They also took the opportunity to reinforce the posts holding up their tents, level the surrounding ground and dig deeper drainage ditches. They hung all that they could out to dry—rags, blankets, mattresses and even foam mats, turning the camps of the displaced into a patchwork of colour against the greyish-white background of their makeshift shelters. But this was the only glimmer of hope on that 1 January, a day when the number of infant deaths from cold hit seven and Israeli bombardments killed twenty-eight people in four separate strikes: fifteen in Jabaliya, in the north, seven east of Gaza City, two in central Gaza, and four in Khan Younis.

The second of January is a holiday in the Gaza Strip. Sixty years ago, in 1965, Fatah—the "Palestine Liberation Movement"—launched its first operation in Israeli territory, in Galilee. The attack only caused material damage to a pumping station, but the commando group managed to return safely to Syria. This infiltration had a considerable impact: the fedayeen, as the Palestinian combatants were known, took up arms to resist both Israel and the Arab regimes. Yasser Arafat, who had founded Fatah with a handful of militants, some of them from Gaza, could proclaim that the "Palestinian revolution" had begun. Four years later, Fatah and the fedayeen took control of the Palestine

Liberation Organisation (PLO), turning an institution that had been under Egypt's thumb into a representative movement.

The PLO initially aspired to replace the state of Israel with a "free and democratic Palestine" giving equal rights to citizens of all faiths. In 1974 Arafat persuaded it to embrace the idea of a "Palestinian Authority" that would govern only the "liberated" Palestinian territory. This was the first time that Palestinian nationalism had shaken off its disastrous "all or nothing" stance, while the Zionist movement had spent decades making gradual advances, leading to the proclamation of the state of Israel in 1948, and then the occupation of East Jerusalem, the West Bank and the Gaza Strip in 1967. A minority of fedayeen, led by the Popular Front for the Liberation of Palestine (PFLP), accused Arafat of having "capitulated" to the "Zionist enemy" and formed a dissident "Rejectionist Front", distanced from the PLO.

In Gaza, Sheikh Ahmed Yassin's Muslim Brotherhood were insisting that it was not military weakness that had lost Palestinians their homeland, but lack of faith. They saw the re-Islamisation of Palestinian society as the absolute priority, rather than any nationalist activism. The Israeli authorities backed the Islamists in order to weaken the PLO, adding fuel to the fire in inter-Palestinian clashes. Pressure continued to build in the Gaza Strip until the first Intifada broke out in 1987. Young activists participating in this "Stone Uprising" refused to resort to arms and, in 1988, pushed Arafat and the PLO to endorse the two-state solution, involving the peaceful coexistence of Israel and a future Palestinian state. Once again, a minority led by the PFLP refused to abandon the armed struggle but, unlike their predecessors in 1974, they did not leave the PLO and agreed to respect collective decisions.

In the face of this pacificist challenge, the Muslim Brotherhood went from one extreme to the other. It ended all collaboration with the occupiers and turned itself into the "Islamic Resistance Movement", known by its Arabic acronym Hamas. It was only Sheikh Yassin's undisputed authority that made such an about-turn possible, since many Islamists feared losing the webs of influence that Israeli goodwill had brought them. Hamas then adopted the demand for the "total" liberation of Palestine that the PLO had just renounced. In 1991 it formed an armed branch in Gaza, the Qassam Brigades, named after the Syrian militant Sheikh Ezzedine al-Qassam, who was killed by the British army in northern Palestine in 1935. In its symbolic tug-of-war with the nationalist PLO, Hamas then espoused a form of Islamist rhetoric dating from before the foundation of the Jewish state whose destruction it sought.

This inter-Palestinian schism worsened in 1993 when Arafat and Rabin signed the Oslo Accords with which each side effectively recognised the legitimate nationalism of the other. But the PLO had to settle for a "Palestinian Authority" (PA) delegated by the occupying Israelis in the territories they had agreed to evacuate, starting with three-quarters of the Gaza Strip. It was to Gaza that Arafat made his triumphant return in 1994, without fully realising that that he had no real sovereignty over an enclave dotted with settlements. Hamas had been founded in Gaza by Islamists who had never left the territory and made much of its local roots compared to the former fedayeen now returning from exile. It also gambled on the failure of the peace process, which it sought to derail through suicide attacks. Arafat spent less and less time in Gaza, preferring Ramallah in the West Bank, which he established as the base of the PA presidency.

Hamas's gamble paid off with the outbreak of the second Intifada in 2000 and the widespread use of suicide attacks. Although Arafat condemned this escalation of violence, in 2002 his presidential palace in Ramallah was placed under siege. He remained there until 2004 and his medical evacuation to France, where he died shortly after. Yassin had been killed a few months earlier by an Israeli strike, leaving both Fatah and Hamas bereft of their historic leaders. Succession in each was decided by contradictory electoral outcomes: Mahmoud Abbas, leader of both Fatah and the PLO, was elected president of the PA with two-thirds of the vote in January 2005, but Ismaïl Haniyeh, head of Hamas, won a large majority in the parliamentary elections a year later.

When it came to electing their president, Palestinian voters opted for continuity in following Arafat with Abbas; but they expressed their rejection of the PA's negligence, not to say corruption, in the parliamentary election. This was unquestionably a vote by default rather than in support. In Ramallah, Abbas wielded the politics of fear with the stated aim of weakening Hamas in Gaza. He rejected Haniyeh's calls for national unity, forcing him to form an Islamist government, which was then boycotted by Western sponsors. In the Gaza Strip, Mohammed Dahlan, a long-time Fatah activist and native of Khan Younis, was head of the powerful PA police and stepped up clashes with the Islamist militias. A simmering civil war soon broke out in Gaza, with as many Palestinians killed by other Palestinians as by Israel.

In June 2007 Dahlan was visiting Egypt and the Qassam Brigades took advantage of his absence to seize control in Gaza. Vicious clashes with every appearance of score-settling involved widespread kneecapping intended to maim and stigmatise opponents for life. Fatah leaders fled to Israel with their families. The split between the PA presidency in Ramallah and the Islamist government in Gaza hardened. Sixteen years of an Israeli blockade only served to deepen the rift. It was now not only two rival leaderships, but two populations—the West Bank and Gaza—that fell out of step, constrained by the occupation to lead parallel existences. Shared holidays such as the 2 January celebration of Fatah are the last remnants of what was once national unity.

Hamas is still claiming to be the sole legitimate "Palestinian Authority" by virtue of its victory in the 2006 parliamentary elections, although its legitimate term in office ended long ago. The mandate given to Abbas is now equally obsolete, yet he has clung on to his presidential office and even dissolved the Palestinian Assembly in 2019. Over the years, Egypt has sponsored several cycles of inter-Palestinian negotiations, all of which hit the stumbling block of Hamas's refusal to disband the Qassam Brigades and the impossibility of combining the rampant bureaucracies of two "Palestinian Authorities". Hamas even adorned its Gaza administration with the title "State of Palestine" following Abbas's symbolic declaration of a "state" at the UN General Assembly in November 2012.

In February 2017 Yahya Sinwar became head of Hamas in Gaza, while Haniyeh went into exile to chair the political bureau, the Islamist leadership abroad. Sinwar had been a founder of the Muslim Brotherhood's armed wing in Gaza, which was targeting their nationalist rivals long before the establishment of the Qassam Brigades. Imprisoned in Israel from 1988 to 2011, he was only released in an exchange of 1,027 Palestinian prisoners for one captive Israeli soldier held by Hamas. He was fluent in Hebrew and spent much of his two decades in prison studying the Israeli security apparatus, dissecting its strengths and weaknesses.

Sinwar was the first leader of Hamas to head both its political and military wings. In May 2017, he endorsed the prospect of a Palestinian state confined to the territories occupied by Israel fifty years before. Like the PLO's revised position of 1974, this was a plan involving coexistence without recognition. Sinwar still refused to negotiate with Israel, choosing instead to not forbid Abbas from undertaking such talks and to accept their conclusions in advance. There was no substance to any of it, as Netanyahu had long ago reduced the scope of discussions with the PA to "security cooperation", primarily against Hamas.

Sinwar was well aware how much Gazans loathed the arbitrariness, brutality and nepotism of Hamas. He was particularly concerned about the election calendar that factions independent of both Fatah and Hamas had managed to impose. Legislative elections in May 2021 were supposed to be followed two months later by a presidential election for which Hamas would not field a candidate. But in April 2021 Abbas, who had pledged not to run again, changed his mind and suspended the entire process. Rather than express opposition to this denial of democracy, the United States and the European Union were relieved that a possible Islamist victory in the West Bank had been avoided. Clearly it mattered little to them that Gazans had been on the verge of ousting the Hamas government.

This proved that the whole world had got used to viewing Gaza solely through the prism of the blockade while pretending to make a few "humanitarian" adjustments. Few still disputed Israel's conflation of the people of Gaza with the organisation that is Hamas. Although Netanyahu lost control of the Israeli government in June 2021, having been prime minister for over twelve years running, in December 2022 he returned to power with the resolute intent to hold onto it, if only to escape the prosecution he faced for corruption, fraud and breach of trust. Absorbed by these self-serving calculations, the prime minister was persuaded he had managed to tame Hamas by facilitating funding from Qatar and providing thousands of permits enabling Gazans to work in Israel.

Sinwar was pleased to have thus lulled the "Zionist enemy" into lesser vigilance. He ordered the Qassam Brigades to stand ready when Israeli aviation targeted their Islamic Jihad allies, and confused the adversary's intelligence agencies with fictional organisational charts for Hamas departments. His secret plan was for his commandos to breach Israeli territory simultaneously in several areas in order to capture a few dozen hostages, while killing the civilians who had not been captured. Following his own release in 2011 in a one-for-one-thousand prisoner exchange, he was convinced he could obtain the release of the some 5,000 Palestinians being held in Israeli prisons. Alongside his Hamas comrades, he wanted to free Marwan Barghouti, Fatah's most popular figure, and Ahmed Saadat, head of the PFLP, who had been held since 2002 and 2006 respectively. Sinwar's ambition was to enshrine Hamas's position at the head of Palestinian nationalism in place of the PLO, which would be indebted to its Islamist rival for the liberation of two iconic officials.

The attacks launched at dawn on 7 October 2023 by the Qassam Brigades and their allies quickly turned into an appalling bloodbath. Three hundred and seventy-eight people were slaughtered at an outdoor music festival. Kibbutzim near the border were the theatre of merciless killing and all manner of violent acts, which the killers filmed and broadcast live on social media. The dregs of Gazan society arriving in the wake of its militias further escalated the horror. Hamas and factions complicit in the atrocities took 251 hostages with them back to Gaza, far exceeding the objective Sinwar had assigned. But this bloodbath, leaving more than 1,200 dead, dealt a terrible blow to the Palestinian cause, linking it to the worst forms of terrorism from which it had long sought to distance itself.

Rather than organise the protection of Gaza's population from inevitable Israeli retaliation, the Qassam Brigades rushed into the tunnels where they had accumulated stocks of water, food, fuel and munitions. They did not recover their pugnacity until Gaza was invaded on 27 October 2023, after which they employed performative urban guerrilla actions to galvanise their base. But the prisoner exchange in late November that enabled a weeklong ceasefire fell far short of Sinwar's expectations. The ratio was in fact one to three, 80 Israeli hostages (and 25 foreigners) released in exchange for 240 Palestinian prisoners, far fewer than the number of Palestinians rounded up by the IDF in the weeks before. And so hostilities resumed with renewed intensity, especially in Khan Younis.

The inability of the international community, and above all the United States, to secure a simple ceasefire has jeopardised the future of Gaza itself. Netanyahu continues to insist on "total victory" over Hamas, while ruling out reinstalling the PA in Gaza for fear that restored ties with the West Bank would breathe new life into the dynamics of a two-state solution. Beyond these slogans, the Israeli government has proved incapable of articulating a clear plan for "the day after" in Gaza. It remains at odds with both its military personnel, who believe they have long since achieved their objectives, and supremacists with their loud calls for resettlement in Gaza—a nightmare scenario for the Israeli General Staff.

Viewed from Gaza on this 2 January 2025, this is an impasse that can only play into the hands of Hamas. The ravages visited upon the Gaza Strip have literally decimated the middle class as well as the intellectual, artistic and academic circles which, as I have seen over the long term, were nurturing both a critical distance from and multifaceted challenges to the rule of Hamas. The civil society alternative to Islamist control has simply sunk into the sea of tents. Day-to-day survival reinforces households' dependence on the clan they belong to, but each clan pursues its local interests and together they have proved incapable of uniting to build a credible counterweight to Hamas.

AN ANNIVERSARY

The once omnipresent green flags of the "Islamic resistance" have vanished from the Gazan landscape. Hamas tolerates a few of the yellow Fatah flags, which are slightly more numerous on this year's anniversary of the 1965 "Palestinian revolution". Passers-by remark ironically that those who own the tent or the shop above which the yellow flag is fluttering hope it will protect them from Israeli strikes. And graffiti on the shore asserts "the Palestinian Authority is a bunch of spies". Those who openly support Fatah explain that their allegiance lies not with Abbas, but with Dahlan. Gaza's former top cop, whom Abbas suspected of plotting against him, was expelled from Fatah in 2011, but retaliated by establishing the "Fatah–Democratic Reform Bloc" to legitimate his own dissidence.

Hamas thus managed to pit one Fatah faction against another, playing Dahlan's supporters against those of Abbas. For a dozen years the Islamists allowed Dahlan to operate from the United Arab Emirates, despite his being a close adviser to the head of state, Sheikh Mohammed Bin Zayed, a harsh critic of the Muslim Brotherhood. Hamas forbade his return to Gaza, but let him delegate to his wife, who organised collective weddings for needy couples in Gaza. The Dahlans subsequently diversified the scope of their generosity, from grants for university students to *in vitro* fertilisation. In 2017 Dahlan was finally able to send his trusted associate Samir Masharawi to Gaza, from which he had been expelled, like Dahlan, ten years prior, in order to put his largesse to greater political use. But Masharawi has remained in Cairo throughout the present conflict, operating in the Gaza Strip through a former mayor of Khan Younis, Osama Al-Fara.

As for the PA under President Abbas, it continues to allocate a portion of international aid to paying the salaries, albeit sporadically, of about 25,000 civil servants in the Gaza Strip. By way of comparison, the Hamas administration employs about 35,000. The PA does not allow its paid officials to work for its Islamist rival, except in the fields of healthcare and education, which it categorises as national interest. Competition between the two parallel bureaucracies, one active, the other technically unemployed, remains the source of recurrent disputes. Both movements refuse to lay off employees, thus keeping hundreds of thousands of people indebted to them, via their extended families. Compounding the issue, Hamas still refuses to disarm the Qassam Brigades.

Representatives of either Fatah faction carry little weight compared to what remains of Hamas. The movement was decapitated when Israel eliminated Haniyeh in Tehran in July 2024, and then Sinwar in Rafah the following October. And the Qassam Brigades, estimated in October 2023 to number 25,000–30,000 combatants, have suffered considerable losses.[1] However, the figure of 17,000 killed, endlessly repeated by Israeli propaganda, makes little sense. It is Netanyahu's way of proving that "total victory" is within reach, with the physical liquidation of over half the Islamist militiamen. This figure also enables him to argue that "terrorists" account for one-third of the victims in Gaza, with, in other words, civilians representing two-thirds of deaths being portrayed as a "reasonable", even "humanitarian" proportion.

Compiling Israel's own sources, the militant death toll is in fact closer to 8,500.[2] But this figure includes combatants from other factions, particularly the Islamic Jihad and the PFLP. And this does not even account for new recruits, whose thirst for revenge has attracted many to the Qassam Brigades. Moreover, Israel uses a very broad definition of Hamas "terrorists" which includes political leaders, administrative officials and police officers. On this 2 January 2025, I wondered how it would classify the traffic officer I saw at an intersection in Khan Younis shouting to break up a traffic jam. Would Israel consider him a "terrorist" simply because he wore the dark blue uniform of the

AN ANNIVERSARY

"Palestinian police", bearing the national coat of arms on the breast of a spread eagle? Yet he was armed only with a whistle, which he wielded with great flair.

The question is not merely rhetorical, because in the early hours of 2 January 2025, an airstrike targeted an Al-Mawasi encampment, killing the Gaza chief of police, Mahmoud Salah, who had been in place for six years, and his deputy, Hussam Shahwan. The fire that engulfed some ten tents produced images that were as shocking as when strikes hit the same "humanitarian zone" on the night of 22 December 2024.[3] A total of twelve people were killed in this bombardment, including three children and two women. The IDF nevertheless claimed to have aimed its strike so as "to mitigate harm to civilians, including using precise munitions, aerial observations and other intelligence gathering". It alleged that Shahwan had "conducted violent interrogations of Gazans, while violating their human rights and persecuting dissidents".[4]

The Hamas interior ministry accused Israel of "spreading chaos" by attacking senior local police officers. Shortly after this, around noon, a missile hit the ministry's headquarters in the Khan Younis municipal building. The cloud of dust and smoke could be seen for kilometres around. The IDF said it had targeted a Hamas "command and control centre", an accusation regularly made to justify strikes on civil institutions, including hospitals.[5] It was nevertheless unable to name even one of the six people killed. The death toll on this public holiday was at least 68, as there had been four other bombings, a significant increase on the daily average of 38 killed in the month of December.

The IDF had prepared the ground for this strike on Khan Younis by dropping leaflets over the preceding days calling on "the noble inhabitants of Khan Younis" to "consign Hamas to the dustbin of history" and to "contact Israeli intelligence", giving WhatsApp, Facebook and Telegram contact details.

It is doubtful that this sort of propaganda would draw many volunteers. In any event, I was soon to measure the attraction Hamas held for young people. Two youngsters of about twelve years of age heckled me at a market stand. They proclaimed their "love" for Hamas, mocking two of their friends as "wimps" and saying that one preferred Fatah, the other the PFLP. They were scrawny and excited, with defiance in their eyes, looking for an enemy to fight.

It was sixty years ago that the "Palestinian revolution" was launched.

WITNESSES

IN THE EARLY HOURS of 3 January 2025, a bomb fell on Omar Dirawi's family home in the north of Deir al-Balah. This twenty-one-year-old photojournalist, who had saved up to buy a camera with his own money as soon as he started university, was a regular contributor to local and international media outlets.[1] The day before, he had been fighting back tears during the funeral for one of his brothers. The strike that cost him his life also claimed the lives of his mother, his father and other relatives. The IDF gave no justification for the strike, which was one of a series of daily bombardments south of the Netzarim Corridor. It was impossible to know whether the invaders intended to widen this military route, which they had already fortified, or if they just wanted to demonstrate their firepower to a terrorised population.

Dirawi became known during the ongoing conflict for travelling all over Gaza to bear witness to the various facets of the tragedy. A selfie on his Instagram account shows him camera in hand, press card around his neck, in his bulletproof vest saying "Press": "This is me today. A survivor of four wars… and a fifth I am waiting for its completion, between the sound of the bombing and the rubble of buildings, the smell of gunpowder and blood, the sight of corpses and body parts, friends disappearing, comrades leaving, and loved ones leaving."[2] Dirawi had survived the wars of 2009, 2012, 2014 and 2021 before this one took him.

Dirawi's blue "Press" vest was placed on his white shroud for his burial in what has become a grim ritual for journalists killed in Gaza. According to the local authorities, he was the 202nd media worker to be killed during this conflict, but already the second in 2025, following the death of another photojournalist, Hassan Al-Qishawi, killed the day before in a drone strike in the west of Gaza City.[3] Twenty-five of the journalists killed were women, including Ayat Khadoura, killed in the bombing of her house in Beit Lahia on 20 November 2023. Two weeks before her death, she had recorded her "last message to the world": "We had very big dreams, but unfortunately, today our dreams are that if we are killed, we are killed in one piece, that people recognise us, that we are not limbs put in a bag."[4]

The New York-based Committee for the Protection of Journalists (CPJ) estimates that at least 136 journalists were killed in the Gaza Strip from October 2023 to December 2024.[5] The CPJ count is lower than the figure quoted locally, owing to a more restrictive definition of professional journalists. The committee nevertheless considers that three-quarters of the journalists killed in the world in 2023 lost their lives in Gaza,[6] and two-thirds in 2024.[7] The CPJ has also condemned the threats made by Israeli officials against Palestinian journalists, some of which have been followed by deadly strikes on the homes of the journalists in question.[8] It is also significant that no journalist killed in Gaza was, according to the CPJ, "caught in the crossfire", whereas these were the circumstances in which many reporters lost their lives elsewhere in the world.[9] In Gaza, there can be no doubt whatsoever: the IDF, and it alone, is responsible for the violent deaths of media professionals.

Reporters without Borders (RSF) has stated that, in 2024, "Palestine has become the world's most dangerous country for journalists", due to both the astounding number of journalists killed or wounded in Gaza and the dozens of journalists being held in Israeli prisons.[10] Between November 2023 and September 2024 RSF filed four complaints for "war crimes" with the International Criminal Court because

"The protection of Gaza's journalists begins with the fight against impunity." The last of these complaints documents the deliberate firing of an Israeli tank on a group of journalists, all wearing their press vests, on 18 August 2024. Ibrahim Muhareb, a 26-year-old reporter, was killed, while his colleagues managed to take cover—by some miracle, as they put it. The IDF did not allow an ambulance to recover Muhareb's body until the next day.

In the high-risk environment of Gaza, one year is worth three and veterans soon become hardened. Two friends, Roshdi Sarraj and Yasser Murtaja, were only twenty and twenty-four when they founded Ain Media—"Eye Media"—in 2012. With one of the first digital cameras in Gaza, Sarraj made videos about the rarely reported daily life of the refugees. The foreign journalists he worked with were surprised to find out that "Gaza could also be such a beautiful place".[11] Murtaja shared his friend's enthusiasm, seizing every opportunity to celebrate life in Gaza in spite of everything. After the war of 2014 between Israel and Hamas, he made a documentary about a five-year-old girl whose face was injured in an airstrike that killed her entire family. The film ends with a message of hope, showing the little survivor's first day at school and her childhood dreams.

On 30 March 2018 young Gazan activists defied Hamas and organised a peaceful march to the border with Israel, instructing participants not to reach it. Tens of thousands answered the call, prompting the Islamists to join the action, concerned that it might turn against them.[12] Murtaja photographed for the international press this "great march of return", which IDF soldiers quashed by firing live ammunition, killing some fifteen marchers. A week later, the second of these marches rallied far fewer demonstrators. Murtaja, as always wearing his "Press" vest, was mortally wounded by fire that RSF described as "clearly intentional".[13] The Israeli defence minister had the gall to accuse the photographer of being a Hamas operative, even though he had been arrested and beaten by the Hamas police three years before.[14] The murderous targeting of Palestinian journalists clearly predates 7 October 2023.

After his best friend was killed, Sarraj carried on with the Ain Media enterprise alone in offices located in the upmarket Rimal district of Gaza City. Foreign reporters who praised his services describe him as "endlessly polite, nonchalantly composed and always meticulous".[15] In early autumn 2023, Sarraj was excited to participate in a *Le Monde* report on the restoration of Wadi Gaza, from which 35,000 tonnes of waste had been cleared to facilitate the regreening of this ancient wetland. The report was published at dawn on 7 October, just before news spread of the horrific Hamas attacks in Israel.[16]

At the time, Sarraj was in the Gulf for a job scheduled long beforehand. He travelled with his wife, Shrouq Aila, also a journalist, and their barely one-year-old daughter. The couple decided to return immediately to Gaza while the crossing with Egypt remained open, because they felt it was their imperative duty to bear witness on site. Rather than return to their apartment, located on the seventh floor of an exposed building, Sarraj thought it best to install his family on the ground floor of his parents' home. He was devastated by the death of one of his agency's photographers, twenty-one-year-old Ibrahim Lafi, killed by an Israeli sniper in the early hours of the conflict, despite his "Press" vest. Sarraj said on social media that despite "the bombing and killing of journalists, […] we are still trying to withstand and continue coverage so the world can see the Israeli crimes in Gaza". He issued an urgent appeal, particularly to the *Washington Post*, for the "international protection" of Gaza journalists.[17]

On 22 October 2023 Sarraj, Aila and their daughter were having breakfast when the family home was bombed. He covered his wife and daughter with his body to protect them. He died instantly, saving his family from being killed but not from being seriously wounded. The moment she was well enough, Aila took over Ain Media and expanded its work with the foreign journalists banned from Gaza. She went to southern Gaza to film the distress of displaced Palestinians in a documentary shown on French television channel M6 in September 2024.[18] Two months later, the CPJ presented her with one of its International Press Freedom Awards. At the ceremony it praised Aila's "independent reporting", saying it "is all the more essential because we, the international press, are not allowed in by Israel", making her and "a handful of Palestinian journalists" the last bulwark to make sure "this censorship does not succeed".

I met Aila on a winter day in Deir al-Balah, not far from her new home. In a pink hijab, sunglasses on her head, she greeted me with a warm embrace. After spending six months in a tent with her daughter, now aged two, she had finally found relatively safe accommodation near international humanitarian workers. She treasures the moments she spends with her child every morning, never sure she'll return to her in the evening. That doesn't stop her from putting her sneakers on to travel the length and breadth of Gaza to find food and to continue reporting. Filming in Khan Younis, only some fifteen kilometres further south, involves arduous journeys, each lasting an hour. Then she must get her bearings in the devastated streets, find scenes and eyewitnesses, capture an intermittent signal and be sure to return home before nightfall.

Aila edits her stories and films, then sends them from Al-Aqsa Hospital in the northeast of Deir al-Balah, which supplies electricity and internet to the local press. She empathises with her colleagues who never leave the hospital compound, too afraid to put themselves at risk, and who spend their days at their computers. But she is clearly driven by a more demanding approach to journalism. She ventures beyond the "humanitarian zone" in her helmet and bulletproof vest emblazoned with the word "Press", despite being convinced that this makes journalists a target for Israeli fire rather than protecting them. With a deeply moving blend of determination and exhaustion, this thirty-year-old widow, raising her daughter alone, repeats she is better off than others. She has collected more than her share of horrifying testimonies. She simply wishes that international solidarity with the journalists killed in Gaza would extend to the orphans they have left behind and to the families of their colleagues who are held in Israeli prisons.

The courage and devotion of Gaza journalists have earned them worldwide admiration and recognition from their peers. In April 2024 the Amsterdam-based organisation, World Press Photo, awarded its highest distinction, Photo of the Year, to Mohammed Salem, a 39-year-old reporter who had worked for Reuters for two decades. He had previously been honoured by World Press in 2010 for the image of a phosphorus bomb launched on Gaza. He was wounded in 2011 by Israeli fire at Erez while covering the release of Palestinian prisoners. His picture featured a Palestinian woman embracing the body of her dead niece, wrapped in a white shroud, at Nasser Hospital in Khan Younis in November 2023. Salem received the prize remotely, from Gaza, and "with humility", glad of the opportunity to bring a wider audience to his image even if it was "not a photo to celebrate".[19] The prize-winning photograph was soon dubbed "the Gaza Pietà".

In September 2024, three Visas d'Or were awarded to Gaza journalists at the Visa pour l'Image festival in Perpignan. The following month, the war correspondents' festival in Bayeux awarded three of its prizes to Rami Abou Jamous for his Gaza diary published on the Orient XXI website from February 2024,[20] and for a documentary to which he contributed.[21] From the tent where he has taken refuge with his family in Deir al-Balah, Abou Jamous dedicated these prizes to his friend Bilal Jadallah, with whom he had founded GazaPress in 2013. For ten years, this institution provided invaluable support for independent journalism in terms of training, equipment and publication. It provided a space of freedom for professionals in the face of Hamas's authoritarianism and a semblance of stability for freelancers with little job security.

On 9 October 2023, GazaPress handed out eighty "Press" vests to journalists who were invited into its office to use electricity and the internet, or just to share a hot meal. But Jadallah was killed a month later by tank fire, on a road that had been declared safe by the IDF. On 10 February 2024 the GazaPress team found its offices had been destroyed following ten days of military occupation in this coastal area of Gaza City. What particularly shocked them was that they had given the building's coordinates to the Israeli authorities and the nearby buildings had been spared. Nine months after the eighty bulletproof vests had been handed out, eleven of the journalists who had received them had already been killed.[22]

Abou Jamous nevertheless managed to open a new GazaPress office in July 2024, this time in an apartment in the north of Deir al-Balah. When we met in the "humanitarian zone" six months later, his calm smile lit up as he described this project. His female colleagues can now make use of a women-only room in the offices, where some of them are also currently housed. Electricity and internet connection are supplied by salvaged solar panels. A specific training course is being set up for press coverage using phones, given the very uneven quality of recordings circulating on social media. The aim is to professionalise these raw testimonies to enhance their credibility, despite the very basic tools and extreme conditions that are the norm in Gaza.

The various forms of pressure exerted by Hamas meant that the preservation of press independence was already a major issue prior to 7 October 2023. And, although its operatives can no longer act as openly as before, they remain just as brutal. The home of Ehab Fasfous, a journalist highly critical of Hamas, was ransacked in Khan Younis by armed men on 6 September 2024. The Palestinian Journalists' Syndicate has criticised "the policy of intimidation and threat" facing some journalists in Gaza without naming Hamas, although there is little doubt who was being referred to.[23] The Palestinian and pan-Arab media still cover this war widely from inside the Gaza Strip. The Arab audience, although less shocked than in autumn 2023, continues to be eager for daily news of the tragedy. The only familiar name in Europe and the United States is Al-Jazeera, which has been the target of several Israeli strikes.

The people I met expressed deep respect for the journalists killed on the job. They were not persuaded by the martial tone of commentaries from Al-Jazeera, which announces "violent clashes" between the invaders and the local "resistance" on a daily basis, when in reality the Israeli war machine faces no more than a handful of guerrilla fighters armed with assault rifles and sometimes rocket launchers. But they spoke very warmly of the journalists who camp out at hospital entrances, tripods unfolded and "Press" vests on, ready to bear witness to the next arrival of dead and wounded. At the least they hope these victims won't meet with general indifference, even if resentment against their Arab and Muslim "brothers" is expressed very bluntly.

I was struck by the often choppy, breathless delivery of journalists reporting live from the Gaza Strip. Their features drawn, gasping for breath, they strive to cram words, facts and tragedies into the time slot they are granted. Only veterans of previous conflicts manage to keep their voices well modulated and their eyes focused, while reeling off a string of horrors with abundant details and statistics. And I remembered the "citizen journalists" I'd seen ten years before, in Aleppo during the Syrian revolution, denouncing the crimes of the Assad dictatorship and its Russian allies.[24] They took incredible risks to bear witness to barbarities so terrible that they could not fail, they hoped, to make the outside world react at last. And then they came to the painful realization that the world from which they hoped so much just went on turning, leaving them to fade away.

That stage of Gaza's descent into hell had been reached well before I arrived. There was no more "media red line", to use the local expression. The bombing of schools and hospitals now elicited no more than carefully calibrated statements of indignation, without proposing any action. So yes, it can happen that men defiled by pain, weeping, bereaved women and families lying in the mud will ask the camera to go away and the reporter to shut up, as there's nothing more to say that hasn't already been said a thousand times. So yes, you walk away, feeling completely powerless and you have to acknowledge that, just as in Syria under the Assads, the victims' words only ring true when presented by a Western reporter.

It's not only the blockade that the Israeli government imposed on the Gaza Strip that summer of 2007, it's also the ban that prevents all Israeli citizens, including journalists, from entering the "hostile entity". The time is long gone when Amira Hass could write *Drinking the Sea at Gaza*, to quote the title of the collection of articles she published while living in the Palestinian enclave from 1993–1996.[25] Even though her colleague Gideon Levy is an authority on Gaza in the Israeli press, he is reduced to conducting interviews with his sources by telephone or on Skype. Now the only Israeli journalists permitted to enter the Gaza Strip are embedded with active combat units. And they are doubtless sincere when they nevertheless claim to have "complete freedom" to work.[26]

Since the massacres perpetrated by Hamas and its allies on 7 October 2023, the IDF has banned foreign reporters from unhindered access to the Gaza Strip. The stark failure of the propaganda operations conducted in mid-November around Gaza hospitals convinced the Israeli government that even "guided visits" might be counterproductive. On 12 December a CNN journalist managed to spend three short hours in the Emirati hospital in Rafah, very close to the Egyptian border, for a report that caused an unusual stir due to being the only one of its kind in the entire conflict. In Paris, I met journalists claiming to return from the "field", when they had only seen Gaza through binoculars from a hill on the Israeli side of the border known for providing the best view of the impact of the shelling.

The Foreign Press Association in Jerusalem filed a petition with Israel's Supreme Court on 19 December 2023, requesting immediate and unrestricted access to the Gaza Strip. Three weeks later, the court categorically rejected this request on the grounds that it could put troops "in real danger", notably by revealing their locations.[27] Since then, despite a series of calls from media groups, institutions and professionals, no foreign journalist has been allowed to enter and work independently in Gaza. European and North American governments, so eager to defend press freedom elsewhere, have not made the slightest attempt to force Israel to lift its total blackout, even in part.

A historian knows from experience that people gradually get used to conflicts that go on and on. It is nonetheless disturbing that the world has become accustomed to the war in Gaza even more quickly than it did to the war in Ukraine. I noted this sad fact on the first day of the year 2024 and can only confirm that it's still the case a year later, but worse.[28] Seen from the Gaza Strip, it is indeed on the media front that Israel has scored its only indisputable victory in this conflict, a victory made all the easier by the fact that the international media have not fought very hard to exercise their right to free information in Gaza. And it has taken the horror of infants dying of cold to arouse a fleeting revival of interest, based on accounts given over the phone, with no direct contact with this abomination.

In this way Gaza's victims are killed twice. First when the Israeli war machine strikes them directly in the flesh or smothers them slowly in their tents. The second time is when the intensity of their suffering and the scale of their losses are denied by the Israeli propaganda, on those occasions when it does not describe them, collectively or individually, as "terrorists". The Western media outlets that have gone along with their exclusion from Gaza continue nevertheless to assert an unlikely balance between the invaders and the populations they are driving back and starving in their own land. And many others still do not give equal treatment to the Palestinian journalists who risk their lives, day in and day out, to inform the world about the hellscape that is Gaza.

In 1972 the photograph known as "the napalm girl" changed the way the American public perceived the Vietnam War, hastening the advent of a peace agreement between the United States and North Vietnam the following year. The photographer who took that picture couldn't have imagined it would have such an impact. He had taken the little girl with third-degree burns to the nearest hospital, thus saving her life.[29] Half a century later, and despite praise from the global community of photojournalists, the "Gaza Pietà" has not launched a debate on a par with its distressing intensity. It's almost as though the ban on Western media in Gaza had deprived the ongoing tragedy of its full universal value. As though the mirror held up to us by women and men in Gaza showed us only our lack of empathy for deaths that no longer feel like our own.

VULTURES

IT'S 2.30 AM, 4 January 2025, and I'm woken by a furious firefight. It's happening a few hundred metres away, on the coast, between the southern edge of the "humanitarian zone" and the Egyptian border. It goes on for a good half hour, accompanied by shouts and screams. For the last three weeks now the IDF has been methodically combing through this "block", numbered 2360 in their classification system for the Gaza Strip. They've gradually driven out the people who had taken refuge there, and in recent nights sent up flares whose dull whistle contrasts with the staccato fire of automatic weapons. They've also destroyed the remaining seafront apartment blocks, which blocked the sight-lines from their ships.

It's a cloudless night and the Israeli drones are back in action, no longer blinded by New Year storms. Their target is the security escort of a convoy of 74 UN-chartered trucks carrying humanitarian aid. This although the IDF itself decided the route, which goes from Kerem Shalom, along the Egyptian border via the Philadelphi Corridor, and then up the coast. And it was also in this sector that, during the night of 22–23 December 2024, a third of the trucks in a humanitarian convey were looted, with drones effectively assisting the looters by killing six guards.[1] The UN had no option but to return to this highly exposed route following the looting of a convoy of 40 trucks going a different way on the evening of 29 December 2024.

Every precaution had been taken that night to protect the trucks, which travelled along the Israeli side of the border with Gaza, from Kerem Shalom to "Gate 96", before coming into the enclave along the Netzarim Corridor. The convoy was protected by Al-Aqsa, a company linked to Egyptian military intelligence. The IDF gave its assent to this "Egyptian" arrangement, and even authorised Al-Aqsa's Palestinian agents to carry weapons. But a few kilometres beyond the end of the corridor, with the inhabitants becoming increasingly aggressive, the guards opened fire, leading to exchanges in which two people were killed. After the confusion died down, only thirteen trucks reached their intended destination, sixteen were looted and found without batteries or tyres, while eleven others "disappeared", which speaks volumes about the scale of local complicity.

This fiasco forced the humanitarian organisations to make another attempt via the coastal route, which led to the ambush that I heard echoing through the early hours of 4 January 2025. The UN accused Israel of launching "a drone strike [that] hit a vehicle from the local community which was protecting part of the convoy".[2] Strikes of this kind only encourage looters, who also clash with the convoy's security guards, while local people hear the noise and rush in to grab something for themselves. In this instance there were eleven people killed, five by the IDF and six in exchanges of fire between Palestinians. Ultimately fifty of the seventy-four trucks were looted, with some of the aid items turning up at Al-Mawasi market the next morning, at a premium, obviously.

A father horrified by these prices he can't afford tells me, "No one steals stuff to sell it for a higher price—except in Gaza". There are no Robin Hoods in Gaza, where criminal gangs grow fat by appropriating humanitarian aid intended for distribution to the general population, or to assist them in other ways. The ever more frequent and organised looting speaks volumes about the collapse of public order in Gaza. Which in turn fuels a shadow war between Israel and Hamas, a merciless war with no frontline, where the UN is caught in the crossfire.

This collapse has much in common with the security chaos that overwhelmed Gaza following the unilateral IDF withdrawal in September 2005. Hamas militants proclaimed the victory of their "Islamic resistance", in increasingly open defiance of Mahmoud Abbas's Palestinian Authority. Gaza's main clans took advantage of the simmering civil war to develop their own criminal autonomy. The Qassam Brigades won the final round, expelling the PA from Gaza in June 2007. The new Islamist authority then turned on the clans, which had grown too powerful, and contained them one by one, with some besieged in their fiefdoms until they surrendered, and others paid off or co-opted.

From the Ottoman period the traditional organisation of Gaza involved a system of mukhtars appointed by each clan, and sheikhs from each of the Bedouin tribes. The role of these men was to settle disputes within their respective groups and promote their own group's interests to the rulers of the day. Both the British Mandate and Israeli occupation regularly tried to use them to counter militant nationalism. In 2007 Hamas suspended the mandates of all the mukhtars and sheikhs, approving only the most docile among them and replacing the others with their own sympathisers. They even authorised the use of customary law rather than sharia to settle some disputes, as long as the procedures remained under their control.

Since 7 October 2023 Netanyahu has endlessly proclaimed his determination to win "total victory" over Hamas, while rejecting the re-establishment of the Ramallah-based PA as the authority in Gaza. The only time he has explicitly mentioned his vision of "the day after Hamas in Gaza", it was to propose handing "civilian management and responsibility for maintaining the public order" to "local elements with managerial experience".[3] In reality this soothing euphemism refers to those clans in Gaza that seem ready to collaborate on a transactional, and indeed criminal basis. However, the first experiment with an arrangement of this kind turned into a nightmare after a week, in what Gazans still refer to as the "flour massacre".

In the early hours of 29 February 2024, a convoy of thirty-three trucks loaded with flour was travelling along the coast road to Gaza City, where for two months no flour had been available at less than a thousand dollars for a 25-kilo sack. The convoy's route was "coordinated" with "private sector providers"—in practice prominent clans from the north of Gaza. The Israelis thought they were killing two birds with one stone—promoting their local partners and slightly easing the suffering of the city's population—while maintaining their offensive further south in Khan Younis. At around 4 am, the convoy was stopped at the military roadblock where the coast road met the road into Gaza. After half an hour it was allowed to go on its way, with an escort of Israeli armoured vehicles.

A huge crowd of some 10,000 anxious civilians had gathered, on the beach and along the road. Their uncontrolled movement in the dark triggered a blood bath. The IDF acknowledges that it "did fire at a number of suspects who approached the nearby forces and posed a threat to them".[4] However, survivors say that they were caught between the fire from Israeli snipers on the beach and from the tanks on the coast road. A total of 118 people were either shot dead, trampled to death in the rush to escape or killed by the convoy, now out of control. As usual, the UN demanded a "rapid, independent and impartial" investigation which, as usual, was never held.

A week after this carnage, US President Joe Biden announced a "massive increase in the amount of humanitarian aid getting into Gaza every day", and ordered the Pentagon to establish a "temporary pier" at the end of the Netzarim Corridor. In coordination with their Israeli counterparts, the American troops had the mission of unloading "large shipments carrying food, water, medicine and temporary shelters". Rather than force Israel to provide land access for aid, the United States had already begun a campaign of dropping humanitarian aid into Gaza from the air, in which they were joined by, among others, the UAE. But then an Emirati military transport plane killed five people in a refugee camp when the parachute on a case of aid failed to open and it "dropped like a rocket".[5]

This tragedy convinced Israel's American and Emirati allies to seek a sea route to get aid into Gaza. On 15 March 2024 an Emirati boat carried 200 tonnes of food from Cyprus for World Central Kitchen (WCK), an NGO founded by celebrated chef José Andrés, who was well-connected in Washington circles, particularly among senior Democrats. WCK had already distributed hundreds of thousands of hot meals in Gaza and intended to expand its operation considerably. However, all the humanitarian organisations agree that there is no real alternative to supplying Gaza through the daily entry of at least 500 trucks, which was the average number until September 2023, particularly if the intent is to provide the "massive increase" that Biden called for.[6]

The day after WCK unloaded a second cargo of food, three vehicles in its convoy were targeted in three successive strikes on the coast road, killing the seven passengers.[7] The Israeli government was forced to admit that this clearly identified convoy had "coordinated" its journey, but said that the sight of an armed man in its proximity had caused this "mistake". It promised it "would adjust" its "practices in the future to make sure this does not happen again". The humanitarian community realised that it was completely vulnerable in Gaza. WCK said its team and operations in Gaza were "targeted deliberately" by Israel, and restarted them a month later with exclusively Palestinian personnel.[8]

Meanwhile, although the cost of the American pier was estimated at over $230 million, it ran into one problem after another. The structure was so heavy and the installation process so complex that the pier did not become operational until 17 May 2024. A week later it was damaged by storms, after which operations were suspended on two separate occasions due to high seas. The damage was repaired in the Israeli port of Ashdod. After a month Washington finally admitted defeat and dismantled the pier, just as the WHO announced that at least thirty-two people had died of hunger in Gaza, including twenty-eight children aged under five.[9]

The situation was made more calamitous because the offensive launched against Rafah on 6 May 2024 had led to the closure of the border crossing with Egypt, further tightening Israel's restrictive grip on Gaza. The number of humanitarian trucks allowed in fell to eighty per day in June and July, then to fewer than seventy in August and fewer than sixty in September. Most of these trucks entered Gaza from the north, via the Erez and Zikim crossings, when most of the population had fled to the "humanitarian zone" in the south. And the highly congested bottleneck at Kerem Shalom led to an area marked on UN maps as a site of "collapse of public order".[10]

Despite the blows it struck against Hamas, Netanyahu and his government had not managed to replace it with any kind of stable coalition of clans opposed to its rule. The clans strengthened their control over the population due to the massive exodus, which forced households that were often displaced more than once to depend more than ever on their larger extended families. These clans provided their members with tents, encampments, distributions of food and water and even contact with international organisations. They retained their meeting places, either in their traditional premises or, when those had been bombed, in a tent. The influence of this organic solidarity can clearly be sensed, for example in the great cemetery in Khan Younis, which remains divided into clan plots, where each bury their own.

However, Israeli manoeuvring to consolidate a clan-based alternative to Hamas did not succeed, because its management of Gaza remained entirely remote. The re-occupation of Gaza was carried out by tanks and armoured vehicles, which drive the residents out, preventing the invaders from creating a web of supporters among the local population, notably in the Netzarim Corridor. The incarceration of thousands of Gazans in Israel serves to recruit informants, if only to avoid abuse, but it does not enable the Israelis to build up a solid network of collaborators.[11] Since the "flour massacre" even relationships formed in Israel with commercial operators in Gaza have remained confined to ad hoc cooperation.

The networks that could have assisted the provision of aid by sea collapsed with the deadly strike against the WCK convoy and the US pier fiasco. The Israeli military took note of their inability to promote a clan-based alternative to Hamas and decided to use organised crime groups more or less overtly. The key figure in this approach was Yasser Abu Shabab, a hitherto minor member of a Rafah clan, whom Hamas had imprisoned in the past for smuggling. But Israeli protection enabled Abu Shabab to substantially expand his activities and to poach around a hundred desperados from other clans. These were often ex-convicts who, like their boss, had been shunned by their families.[12] Abu Shabab's gang, as it must be called, operated in full view of the IDF, just the other side of the Kerem Shalom crossing, and sported brand new weapons, an irrefutable clue to its collaboration with the occupiers.

Abu Shabab's rise went hand in hand with Israeli propaganda operations seeking to pin all responsibility for the humanitarian crisis in Gaza on the UN, on the grounds that it was incapable of effectively distributing the aid that

Israel claimed to have generously allowed in. The reality was that October 2024 saw the number of humanitarian aid trucks admitted fall to fewer than forty per day, the lowest level since the start of the conflict a year earlier. In addition, as soon as these trucks left Kerem Shalom, they were at the mercy of attack from Abu Shabab's gang, which openly patrolled this highly dangerous sector. It was not until 12 November that the IDF reopened the Kissufim crossing further north, and with it a shorter, less exposed route to the "humanitarian zone" of Al-Mawasi.

In October 2024 40 % of international aid trucks were looted shortly after coming in through Kerem Shalom.[13] Twice, on 8 and 15 October, Israeli drones targeted the escorts of the convoys while sparing the looters, who had no hesitation in attacking and even killing the drivers. The Israeli military justified these strikes in the name of a "no weapons" policy, which they clearly did not apply to the Abu Shabab gang. Private convoy organisers were compelled to disarm their escorts, who were then equipped only with sticks, and were forced to pay the looters exorbitant "protection" money of $3,500–7,000 per truck. This vicious circle of organised crime led to a spectacular rise in the prices of necessities in Gaza's markets, which then encouraged ordinary civilians to take part in organised looting, for either their own personal consumption or resale.

The reopening of the Kissufim crossing did not bring the hoped-for respite. The first convoy allowed in, on 12 November 2024, did not lose a single truck. However, the following day, 500 metres after leaving Israeli soil, fourteen of the twenty trucks in the convoy were looted and three drivers shot and injured. The UN decided to return to the Kerem Shalom crossing for a convoy of 109 trucks carrying emergency food aid, scheduled to enter Gaza at dawn on 17 November. The UN obtained assurances from the IDF that the route had been secured and, to foil the looters, the convoy set off five hours before the scheduled departure time. Nevertheless, only eleven trucks got through unscathed, before the ones behind had their tyres shot to deliver them up to the clearly well-informed criminals. The unarmed escort could offer no resistance to the looters who, despite the assault rifles they carried, were clearly viewed with indulgence by the Israeli soldiers stationed not far away. The ninety-eight hijacked trucks were promptly driven to sites where forklift trucks were waiting to unload them.[14]

The flour would have provided bread to southern Gaza for a week and its theft forced the World Food Programme (WFP) to use up its reserves to prevent the bakeries from closing. On 18 November 2024 Hamas responded by killing at least twenty of Abu Shabab's henchmen, including his own brother. The local authorities declared this an operation against "criminal gangs", carried out by "the security forces in cooperation with tribal committees".[15] Hamas police deployed their black-scarved, sometimes hooded commandos, known as Saham ("arrow"), to do the job, and compelled some clan members to act alongside them, or at least to approve the operation.

This demonstration of force led the Netanyahu government to become increasingly overt in its targeting of food aid convoy security teams, in the name of "total victory" over Hamas. On 12 December 2024 the Israelis carried out two successive airstrikes, in Rafah and then in Khan Younis, on the escort for a convoy taking flour to UN warehouses. Twelve security staff were killed in these strikes, while civilians rushed to the overturned trucks to grab flour. The combination of a starving population and profiteers selling their loot on the black market ensured that confusion reigned, while the IDF continued to take all the "humanitarian" credit for convoys it had simply allowed into Gaza, accusing the UN of incompetence in aid distribution, and even of complicity with Hamas.

A HISTORIAN IN GAZA

Arriving in the Gaza Strip a week after this event, I found people constantly fearful of both Israeli airstrikes and looters. The UN convoy I travelled in from Kerem Shalom had first to pass through the hunting grounds of Abu Shabab and his gang. This meant we had to don helmets and bulletproof vests before climbing into armoured 4x4s that set off into the night. And it was only once we reached the "humanitarian zone" that we could take them off and get into "soft" vehicles, as the security staff call vehicles without any specific protection.

Over the years of my regular visits to Gaza, I have gathered many accounts of dispossession and flight, bombings and injuries. But I have never heard so many stories of looting in such abundant and sordid detail. Every day in late 2024 brought me tales of gangs attacking humanitarian convoys, makeshift roadblocks and children clinging to trucks to make off with a sack or two of flour. Abu Shabab's gang, protected by Israeli goodwill southeast of Rafah, had imitators even in the "humanitarian zone". One early afternoon a group of around six hooded men armed with a pistol, six grenades and, improbably, a scalpel, held up vehicles south of Deir al-Balah. North of the town after nightfall, there were rumours of a second attack following a strike by an Israeli drone to keep the roads empty, making it easier to burgle the warehouses.

Israeli bombing enabled thousands of criminals to escape from prisons whose walls were breached. In the chaos of Gaza, their predatory brutality was their greatest asset. Those that did not join an existing gang picked through the ruins, making off with any remaining furniture, solar panels and domestic equipment. Sometimes they were simply finishing off the stripping started by Israeli soldiers who had occupied an apartment, leaving its walls covered in Hebrew graffiti. In Deir al-Balah there was even a "thieves' market" where useful items could be bought on the cheap, with no illusions as to the criminal origins of the wares for sale. Blue gas canisters that had been painted to hide the owner's name were euphemistically known as "coloured canisters".

One by one, taboos were broken in a society that had hitherto been conservative and protective. Women, the vast majority wearing the hijab, left their traditional handbags at home in favour of a small rucksack that was harder for thieves to snatch. Gangs of barefoot street children in patched clothes, with grimy, blackened faces, hung around begging at roundabouts, punching cars as a means of persuasion. The clans were undermined by disputes over the distribution of the few wages and the sharing of aid, which led to clashes between them. Never a day passed without the sound of automatic gunfire, soon identified as "family quarrels". A quick check and everyone got on with their lives, since the risk of getting accidentally injured in a "family" argument was less than in an Israeli airstrike.

Also daily, and always unbearable, were the stories and images of kneecappings. Hamas systematically and publicly used this punishment which, during the civil war of 2007, it had reserved for its Fatah enemies. Now it was used to punish looters, or those whom a parody of justice had identified as such, mutilating them for life. Masked militiamen would drag their victim into the street and shoot them point blank in the knee, filmed by a hooded accomplice. The images were quickly uploaded to social media, including a collective punishment where, one by one, ten torturers shattered the knees of prisoners bound at their feet. In the hospitals the numbers of those injured in Israeli airstrikes was now briefly matched by those resulting from inter-Palestinian violence.[16]

Fifteen months after the war started, Netanyahu and his government stated that "the political solution to Gaza is not relevant to the issue of the plan and the activity required now".[17] Paradoxically, this Israeli attitude played into the hands of Hamas, which portrayed itself as preserving what remained of order in a context of rapacious looting. But Hamas had clearly been weakened by the elimination of its historical leaders and most exposed senior personnel, who all had political experience. The liquidation of this hierarchy left a void that was quickly filled by members of the rank and file who until then had been mere enforcers. In Gaza these heavies have long been known as *zanzanas*—"drones"—reflecting their constant, brutal intrusions into the homes of their fellow citizens. The invaders' blindness has handed over the territory to these Islamist shock troopers, who are more inclined to deliver beatings than sermons.

The chaos unleashed by Israeli support for the looters led the UN to note "a dangerous pattern of sabotage and deliberate disruption":

> Israeli forces are unable or unwilling to ensure the safety of our convoys. Statements by Israeli authorities vilify our aid workers even as the military attacks them. Community volunteers who accompany our convoys are being targeted. There is now a perception that it is dangerous to protect aid convoys but safe to loot them.[18]

The Gaza I knew, so concerned to uphold its honour, has become a place where crime pays.

DEATH

IN GAZA DEATH NOW can come at any time. It appears on the family calendar at whim, taking the young before their elders, striking both at night and in broad daylight, after an ultimatum or without warning, on an open road, in a market, between two tents, at the entrance to a "corridor", because he turned down that road, because she didn't, because they went out, because they stayed home. Death has moved in everywhere, from the "blocks" to be evacuated to the "humanitarian zone", from the homes people cling to beyond all reason to the refuges where they once believed in international protection. But this is not the death of past tragedies and wars. No, this is a different, insatiable death; it is mutant and monstrous.

Before, you'd meet death in the proud eyes of the "martyred heroes", with whose portraits every faction, starting with Hamas, stamped the sacrifices of their own people on urban areas. Today these posthumous effigies have gone, aside from the odd yellowed poster in an alleyway, because portraits need walls to be posted on. Now it's "child martyrs" whose presence under the rubble is indicated by their names scratched into a block of cement and, sometimes, by a touching sketch of their face. Thousands lie buried under the ruins—they are the "disappeared" of all ages, for whom civil defence teams and distraught parents have sought in vain, lacking even the consolation of retrieving their bodies.

Once, death was given its rightful time and place. The body was carefully washed, groomed and purified. It was wrapped in a triple-layered white shroud. Family and friends would gather to hear prayers said with feeling and respect. There were then three days for them to receive condolences and begin their mourning. Today's death throws widows and orphans at the dark faces of hospitals, where death is registered, made official, where the body is left, washed, wrapped in a white sheet—quickly, too quickly, because so many other bodies are waiting and because time and space are limited.

The "Morgue and Washhouse Building" as it is officially titled, is more usually called the "bodies refrigerator". Devastated people sometimes spend the whole night there, resting their heads against the wall of the building, weeping for the relative they have had to let go without a vigil. To avoid this ordeal, refugees living in tents get together to pay for their own "washhouse for the dead", even if it's in the sand dunes. And once the body has been returned, after a last embrace, a final kiss, the stretcher is taken up, a cloth is placed over it and it is carried quickly, too quickly, to the nearest cemetery.

And this is when the new death appears for all to see. Because before—just yesterday—there would have been silence as the corpse passed by; conversations would have ceased, to honour even a stranger, and perhaps to join the procession to the burial site. Today people automatically step aside, they prefer to look away, they already have so much pain to bear, they are suffocating from so much repressed mourning. Where once they felt solidarity and unity, now they must struggle for the basic minimum to keep their own children alive and they rely on those closest to them to shoulder this terrible responsibility. Their horizons have been reduced to those of the tent or room they find themselves living in. And like Ayat Khadoura in the hell of Beit Lahia, their only dream is to die "in one piece".

For the new death feeds on what were once unimaginable nightmares. Whole families wiped out at once by a single bomb, heaped in a mass grave and buried by bulldozer.[1] The mass graves opened in hospital grounds—once the siege has been lifted—

where attempts must be made to identify bodies as the season turns to a stinking spring.[2] The cemeteries opened up by the invading bulldozers of the Israelis, who plead negligence and deny intending to use them in exchanges of bodies.[3] The containers sent back from the Israeli side, loaded with anonymous, often decomposed bodies, sometimes several wrapped together, shunned first by a hospital that deliberately closes its doors and then by a humanitarian organisation that likewise wants no part in anything so vile.

The old death still enabled surviving relatives to guide their nearest and dearest into a shared future; this new death crushes mothers and fathers—not every mother and father maybe, but far too many children witness the crushing of their fathers and mothers. Fathers because they couldn't prevent all this uprooting, flight, cold, hunger and fear. Mothers because no matter what they do with the leftovers, the meals have no taste, even when every mouthful is chewed over and over again. And how can you breastfeed a baby when you're exhausted, depressed and have an empty stomach? How can you provide powdered milk when you are destitute? How can you give a bit of warmth when you yourself are chilled to the bone?

Today's death has cast the children from the schools, most of which have been destroyed or damaged.[4] A whole generation feels betrayed by the schools, which have stopped providing education, or even protection from war. In July 2024 alone, 270 people, many of them children, were killed in the bombing of schools housing refugees.[5] And when the summer of 2024 came to an end, there was no new school year for the 57,000 children who were only now old enough and joined the 658,000 others who had been deprived of education for over a year.[6] A third of Gaza's population, the youngest third with the most to offer, has been prevented from going to school.

Of course, by way of a palliative there are the "education tents" erected on a pavement in Deir al-Balah or at the foot of a dune in Al-Mawasi. Dozens of children are sorted into three levels and supposedly learning a bit more Arabic, maths and English. Although these tents have names like "Success" and "School", and their teams are devoted and attentive, what they provide is more entertainment than teaching. And, except for the centres run by UNICEF, enrolment is not free. So school textbooks end up on market stalls, their pages torn out to wrap falafel and sweets.

The children of the old Gaza had school uniforms and school bags. Almost half of them attended schools run by UNRWA, the UN agency for Palestinian refugees, whose activities Israel decided to ban at the end of January 2025. So now the new death accompanies street children in their wanderings. The open-air rubbish dumps they pick through for paper, cardboard, nylon—anything they can use to make a fire and get a little warmth. The taps to which they drag jerrycans almost as big as they are. The dusty roadside stalls, where they harass the customers, swearing like troopers, where they measure out flour in a dish, holding the sack tight between their skinny legs, and where they peddle bits and pieces they've found here and there, maybe in the sandy streets, where they run in bunches towards a new distribution point, with blackened pots on their heads.

For months UNICEF has said that almost all the children in Gaza are in urgent need of psychosocial and mental health support.[7] Psychotherapy of any kind is out of the question during the hostilities, for fear of cracking the armour that helps them survive and keep going. And the same is true for the adults. In any case there are only four psychiatrists in the entire enclave, one in Gaza City, two in the "humanitarian zone" and one in Rafah. There are around ten psychologists—in reality medical students in their first or second year of specialisation. So psychological support is provided by social workers in dedicated sections at hospitals and clinics.

This is one of the services offered by the Nasser hospital in Khan Younis, on one side of an inner courtyard with a few trees and a fountain. Posters showing a smiling figure say "Talking about your problems makes you stronger" and "You are not alone, we are here for you". I meet two clowns dressed in yellow, pink and green: a man of short stature with a tambourine and his partner in a green beret. Their buffoonery and red clown noses eventually raise a smile from an injured infant. They come here once a week, and the rest of the time they entertain children in the camps of the displaced. The hospital regularly brings in a puppet theatre and a guitar player. And soap bubbles are a way of bringing back play and laughter. Drawing can also give comfort to children, if only because choosing colours offers them some element of control over their lives.

For my *Gaza: A History,* I conducted a long interview with Eyad Sarraj, a prominent nationalist figure and pioneer of Palestinian psychiatry, who died in 2013. The Gaza Community Mental Health Programme he founded in 1990 works closely with refugees who do not dare or cannot go to a hospital. In Deir al-Balah a social worker from the programme spoke to the mother of a twelve-year old who had stopped speaking and eating after two of his friends had been killed in front of him three days earlier. After a long silence, the boy burst into tears. "They said my friends would go to Paradise. But one of them was found with no head. How can he go to Paradise without his head?" The social worker managed to calm the boy and persuade him to eat.[8]

A local psychologist explains that the truth, no matter how cruel, is crucial in enabling traumatised children to begin to absorb shock. Some families think they need to protect young victims, and aid their recovery if they are injured, by not telling them about the deaths of their loved ones. But such a painful secret, with the anxiety attached, can nurture a lasting feeling of guilt. In Gaza where, on average, around a hundred people have been killed every day since October 2023, "survivor guilt" leaves deep scars.

The UN speaks of a "war against children" in Gaza, noting that more "children have been killed there in recent months than in four years of conflict worldwide".[9] On 13 August 2024, Mohammed Abu al-Qumsan learned of the deaths of his three-day-old twins in the bombing of Deir al-Balah, just a few minutes after he had registered their births. On 16 September the Hamas Ministry of Health published a list of identified deaths, validated by the Palestinian Authority in Ramallah. On 115 of its 649 pages, the document lists the names of children under ten. The first victim aged over eighteen appears 100 pages later.[10]

On this basis, at the very end of 2024 the number of children killed in Gaza was estimated to be nearly 15,000, or around a thousand per month. The number of wounded children long ago rose over 35,000, an appalling proportion of them mutilated. A third of the some 10,000 bodies buried under rubble are thought to be children. A recent analysis of trauma data concludes that the Ministry of Health data is an underestimate—by 41 %.[11] While it is hard to put the horror of Gaza into words, statistics do not necessarily provide a more reliable indication of the ongoing slaughter, as the figures are so disturbing they upset even the people who produce them.

In February 2024, the UN stopped updating their estimate of 19,000 orphans in Gaza,[12] and even reduced it slightly to 17,000 or 18,000.[13] This uncertainty is a direct consequence of the hostilities, as UNICEF's distribution of identification bracelets to the youngest children, which began in April 2024, was abruptly ended a month later by the Israeli offensive on

Rafah.[14] And it is no longer possible to depend on orphans being looked after by an uncle or cousin. It is already extremely hard for families to survive several forced displacements, not to mention the difficulty of transportation within the Gaza Strip. Where possible, hospitals look after young injured children unclaimed by any relative until they can hand them over to a neighbour or volunteer family.[15]

The tragedy of orphans in Gaza flows on from the distressing figure of 10,000 women killed during this conflict. And the pregnant women who survive have sometimes had to give birth in appalling conditions, particularly when some hospitals are under siege. The average of 180 births per day in Gaza in October 2023[16] had fallen to 130 a year later.[17] The rate of stillbirths reached 12 % in September 2024 with 28 % premature births. More than nine out of ten women suffer from UTIs, a catastrophic situation only partly explained by the shortage of drinking water. The lack of sanitary facilities worthy of the name in tent cities and overcrowded shelters means that women often prefer not to drink.

The disastrous degradation of hygiene hits women harder than men. They are twice as likely to get skin infections and make up two-thirds of those suffering from hepatitis A and gastro-intestinal infections, probably related to their essential role in caring for the sick.[18] The calamitous lack of sanitary protection makes things even worse for around 700,000 women in Gaza, who have to use simple rags. And washing this makeshift protection is not so easy, given that three-quarters of them have no access to clean water. Not drinkable water, just clean.

The descent into hell of Gaza's women could end there. But in May 2024 the UN raised the alarm regarding the growing exposure of women and girls in Gaza to sexual and sexist attacks.[19] The confinement of so many people in the so-called "humanitarian zone" had brought them into even closer contact, with all the attendant risks and blurred lines this entailed. The taboo on reporting domestic violence began to crumble. In front of his children in a tent in Khan Younis, a violent husband expressed his deep shame and "helplessness", before going on to apologise to his entire family. His abused wife found a little comfort in psychological support groups, where she felt less alone in her misfortune.[20]

Sexual violence became so serious that in October 2024 the Ministry of Health set out the procedures to be followed in cases of rape, with abortion "facilitated" until the 120th day of pregnancy. After that date there was a great deal of pressure for the situation to be regularised by marriage. Some families, terrified by the lack of privacy in their makeshift shelters, decided to marry their daughters as soon as possible to give them some form of protection. These unions were imposed on the girls and hurriedly conducted without the least celebration. With the new death that had overtaken Gaza, marriage seemed to have become just another survival reflex.

Even when the longed-for ceasefire finally comes, the new death will remain unsatisfied. In the spring of 2024 the density of the ruins had risen to over 100 kilogrammes per square metre, with a volume of debris comparable to that accumulated throughout the war in Ukraine, in an area 1,600 times smaller.[21] The amount of asbestos contaminating this sea of rubble is inexorably nearing 1 million tonnes, while the destruction of most of the solar panels has leaked very dangerous quantities of lead and cadmium into the porous ground, threatening to pollute the water table still further. Meanwhile the thousand tonnes of waste generated daily in the encampments piles up in unregulated, open dumps or is slowly burned.

This is the highly degraded environment in which Gaza's children go on smiling, running and playing hide-and-seek, rolling marbles and spinning tops. Yet widespread pollution is not the worst danger they face. The IDF estimates that 10–15 % of the bombs it has dropped on Gaza did not explode. Its only concern is to prevent these tonnes of munitions from falling into the hands of Hamas, for which they are the main source of military supplies.[22] But the unrecovered explosives are also, and literally, an abundance of time bombs. For this reason, the International Red Cross has created giant frescos warning children not to climb on the ruins and never to touch a lethal device that looks like a toy. Along the edge of one of these frescos is what is meant to be a positive message:

"Every challenge is an opportunity to develop."

For now, the main beneficiary of Gaza's many "opportunities to develop" is death.

INGENUITY

ON THE MORNING OF 12 January 2025 north of Gaza City, two civilians were killed by Israeli soldiers who deemed them a threat. In reality they had just entered a highly exposed zone to gather firewood. Their bodies were evacuated to Al-Ahli hospital, where their deaths were registered, and added to the twenty-six others reported that day—a minimum total due to the intermittency of telecommunications networks and the dangers faced by ambulances operating without any clear front lines. In the period 3–10 January the UN identified 527 acts of war by the Israelis (208 air strikes, 143 artillery bombardments, 142 instances of fire from machine guns and automatic weapons, 24 bombardments and firing from the sea and 10 ground incursions) and 6 rockets fired by Palestinians.[1] It is what could be described as a one-way war.

In the absence of electricity and fuel, firewood has become a highly valued commodity. Each successive wave of hostilities and displacements brings the savage felling of surviving trees. In order to gather logs and twigs one must now get as close as possible to the Israeli lines. In what was for millennia a prosperous oasis, the last areas of palm trees, olive trees, orange trees and guava trees have been carefully fenced off. Wood that is still green is no longer left untouched and carts are piled high with leafy branches. Along the Salah al-Din Road charcoal burners tend smoking heaps and sell bags of carbonised wood to a select few drivers.

The coast road sellers recover very small amounts of this charcoal. They must then wear themselves out chopping up stubbornly resistant trunks and knotty stumps to sell off as kindling. Even such poor quality wood is more expensive than the dismantled pallets and cannibalised planks that end up in flames. People prefer it to the plywood panels, doors and furniture legs that are sold to the highest bidder. Amid this general fragmentation, Gaza still has its focused, conscientious carpenters who put the finishing touches to their work in wobbly tents, even as, just a few sandy metres away, tables, chairs and desks are painstakingly dismantled.

Wood from all sources is used to fuel clay ovens built on the ground, fanned by coughing women. And when wood is hard to find, they keep their fires going with bits of cardboard and fabric gleaned by children from the nearest dump. No one wants to sink so low and they try not to, sometimes with success. But in the face of great scarcity you have to make do. At least they haven't had to resort to begging, so they bustle in the soot and smoke. Oil drums converted into braziers are not necessarily any more sheltered from the wind. One community canteen recycled washing machine drums as a more effective way to contain fire and retain its heat.[2]

The small quantity of fuel allowed into Gaza is brought in by humanitarian convoys that are severely restricted by the IDF. Its allocation prioritises health services, water desalination and distribution, and running the few bakeries. Any smuggled fuel brought in is not additional to this supply but obtained simply by looting those same convoys. It is then transported and sold on the black market, in tanker trucks stolen by the looters, which are thus lost to the humanitarian organisations that so sorely need them.

On 9 January 2025, the Israeli military boasted that on the three preceding days it had allowed "6,750 liters of fuel, 10,000 liters of water, dozens of food crates and nearly 300 boxes of

INGENUITY

medical supplies" into Gaza. While this was presented as "large quantities of humanitarian aid to several hospitals", it is clearly a negligible amount for over two million people.[3] The fuel provided in those three days would barely cover the consumption of a single hospital like the Al-Aqsa in Deir al-Balah. And this delivery much trumpeted by Israel was approved only after alarm calls from Gaza about the risk that vital hospital services were about to cease.[4]

The figures are inexorable: as long as Israel continues to allow in only a tenth of the humanitarian aid that entered before the conflict, Gaza will go on hovering on the brink of collapse. Even priority services for health, water and bread receive only emergency provision, with fuel reserves never covering more than two weeks. With these essential services so deprived, the population have embarked on a paradoxical energy transition. As the price of diesel is sky high, most of the vehicles it once fuelled now run solely on vegetable oil, usually sunflower, a last resort that will wear them out in a couple of years.

Aside from the fuel nomenklatura and vegetable oil daredevils, anything in Gaza that moves around on wheels does so using either bottled gas or animal traction. Donkeys and horses pull carts laden with water containers, firewood and passengers sitting back to back, dangling their legs over the sides. This public transport is the cheapest, but also the type that most blocks the roads of the "humanitarian zone", due to its frequent stops and laborious manoeuvring. Most motorised vehicles get their energy from a bottle of "cooking gas" wedged in the front of a three-wheeler, tied to the luggage rack of a motorcycle, slipped into a car boot or slotted under its gear box.

It would be hard for me to explain how these arrangements work. All I know is that, what with vehicles drip-fed gas and the constant flow of displaced people moving between the tents, you seldom get up to more than 15 kilometres an hour on the coast road. And along the way you encounter children guarding scales to gauge the volume of a canister's contents by weight. The Gazans seem to have fully mastered this salvage technology, since I heard no reports of gas-related traffic accidents throughout my stay, though there were many tragedies in tents where a brazier was tipped over or a fire not properly put out.

At the roadsides you see adverts for "charging points". These are often no more than a tent with a plank for a counter and a solar panel set at an angle in the sand. This energy source provides 12 volts of direct current, enough to revive the phones that clients leave there for an hour or two. Better equipped shops manage to recharge batteries that can then run on alternative current using a transformer. Then there are the sellers of phone credit, who need only a chair and a box, with a choice of the two Palestinian operators, Jawwal and Ooredoo (whose controlling shareholder is a powerful Qatari group).

Phone numbers in the Gaza Strip are all Israeli, with the 972 code and interception facilities to match. Most fresh produce also comes from Israel, although goods tend to be attributed with West Bank origins. Imports from Egypt have become rarer since the Rafah crossing was closed in May 2024. These days clothes and tools "made in China" come through Israel, ranging from very low-quality Gucci and Cardin fakes to dull synthetic djellabas and bright pink plastic flip-flops.

All transactions in Gaza are made in Israeli shekels, from a tasty treat bought for small change in the street to wholesale contracts between cross-border operators.[5] Thirty years ago Harvard scholar Sara Roy applied the concept of "de-development" to this enclave dominated over the long term by the Israeli economy, which then benefits from a low-cost local workforce and sells its products to a captive market.[6] Such multifaceted dependence constituted a structural obstacle to authentic development in Gaza, while the Strip's standard of living was indexed to the number of work permits for Israel granted by the occupiers.

This downward spiral could have been overturned in 2005, with the withdrawal of the IDF and thousands of settlers. At the G7, former World Bank president James Wolfensohn presented a plan for the resolute development of a Gaza open to the world, through the expansion of its port and reopening its airport, demolished by the IDF in 2001. But this plan, with an estimated cost of 3 billion dollars, came up against Israel's refusal to negotiate the terms of evacuation with the Palestinian side. This refusal inevitably weakened the PA, to the benefit of Hamas, which took over in Gaza in June 2007.

After this, the Israeli blockade of Gaza enabled Hamas to stifle those private entrepreneurs who still dared to defy it, and to bring most of the local economy into its sphere of influence, where necessary by force. Gazans call this domination by Hamas under Israeli occupation the "nightmare within the nightmare". The occupation itself, though now managed remotely, remained as oppressive as ever. But the "de-development" of Gaza was made worse because, after each cycle of hostilities between Israel and Hamas, financial backers promoted the same form of "reconstruction".

The conference that met to that end in Cairo in August 2014 garnered commitments amounting to 5.4 billion dollars, compared to the 3 billion proposed by Wolfensohn nine years before for a development plan of far greater ambition than simple reconstruction. Moreover, the financial backers had no direct hold over a territory in the grip of Hamas, which prioritised its own supporters in the allocation of international aid and actively hindered its distribution to potential opponents. Then there were the demands of the Israelis, who slowed down the whole process, and the right of veto given to the PA, which strove to maintain its own client networks in Gaza. That is why this "reconstruction" programme, so generously endowed in Cairo in 2014, had achieved only some of its main goals by October 2023 and still had a long way to go.

Gaza would offer an extraordinary field study to any economist fascinated by price fluctuations. Supply is strictly limited by the IDF, and depends on commercial operators and also looters who misappropriate humanitarian aid. Larger traders tend to delocalise, mainly to Egypt, to escape the effects of widespread violence. When Israel opens an access point, this encourages prices to fall in the nearest market—Gaza City for Zikim, Deir al-Balah for Kissufim and south of the "humanitarian zone" for Kerem Shalom. Products delivered to the north of the Strip remain blocked by the Israeli barrier that is the Netzarim Corridor, while goods available first in Deir al-Balah soon reach the markets of Al-Mawasi, and vice-versa, but at higher prices linked to internal transportation.

On 2 January 2025 there was great excitement in Deir al-Balah at the arrival of the first loads of chicken seen for months. The price at that time was 200 shekels a kilo—exorbitant for Gaza—as buyers feared the delivery would be a one-off. The next day the price dropped to 150, before settling at around 30–40 after a week of sustained deliveries, with a supplement south of the "humanitarian zone", which was further from the point of entry to Gaza. Employees with a moderate but regular income could afford the relative luxury of a dinner of chicken maftoul, the Palestinian couscous. But most of the population bore the full weight of the quadrupling of prices for everyday goods and were dependent on aid for their survival.[7]

The alarming inflation of the occupier's currency is even more evident for the "cooking gas" that has become such a crucial fuel for transportation. It is true that the official price of a 12-kilo

INGENUITY

gas canister has only gone up from 60 to 70 shekels. However, to purchase at that kind of price your name has to be on a humanitarian distribution list, which provides for eight canisters per month per family at this subsidised rate. The distribution itself is irregular and the gas often sells out. Meanwhile the same canisters cost at least 500 shekels a piece on the black market, excluding most potential clients. People settle instead for a modest 1 or 2-kilo canister to meet their daily needs, as do drivers of the various vehicles that run on "cooking gas". This involves transferring the gas from a larger canister to a smaller one, a service for which a fee is charged. Bills for cooked food and transportation reflect the considerable costs of gas.

Access to valuable shekels is a major thing in itself, as every bank and bureau de change in Gaza is now closed. The brand-new notes I bring in from Amman are greeted with joy by my local grocers, even the new 200-shekel notes, said to be harder to spend. Used notes, on the other hand, are closely examined and sometimes rejected by a suspicious trader, particularly red 20-shekel notes, which are the most common. Of course, no one in Gaza knows that the Bank of Israel chose to illustrate this note with a portrait of the poet Rachel Bluwstein, who died in Tel Aviv in 1931, long before the state of Israel was founded.

This mistrust has fostered the emergence of specialist "note repairers" who, for 0.5 % commission, work wonders with the most damaged note and jealously guard the secrets of their craft.[8] Meanwhile 10-shekel coins with their bronze palm trees are always rejected. Blackened by too much use, their appearance dissuaded shopkeepers before leading to a widespread boycott. However, 1, 2 and 5-shekel coins are spared such discredit, being protected by their tough, silvery alloy of copper and nickel.

The lack of cash is good news for the moneylenders who have replaced the hundred or so ATMs functioning in Gaza

135

before the conflict. These lenders will provide large shekel notes in exchange for a bank transfer plus a commission that reflects the quality of the notes. In November 2024 this was still 25–30 %, but it has since fallen to 12–14 %. Electronic payment has become the norm for retailers who can use it to pay their suppliers. The most popular app belongs to the Bank of Palestine, which has its headquarters in Ramallah. Clients simply pay a bank transfer fee, rather than overpriced commission. But the cash crisis remains, driving some to sell off their family's gold jewellery for less than $2,300 per ounce when the price was three times higher before the conflict.

Northeast of the "humanitarian zone", Deir al-Balah— the "date palm monastery" in Arabic—has been regularly targeted by Israeli airstrikes. Though each destroys an apartment block, or even a whole row of houses, there is not the same devastation as that inflicted by the invasion of Khan Younis and Rafah, or the Israeli pounding of Gaza City. Still Deir al-Balah does not look like a real city. The built environment is disfigured and mutilated, while its pavements, squares, remains of gardens and even its cemeteries have been taken over by tents, with only the spaces between them left to accommodate future arrivals of the displaced. Still it is a city, with a few bakeries and discreet warehouses—but a city in *trompe-l'œil* where canvas stalls have more stock than solid supermarkets.

After long months languishing in tents, refugees build shelters out of beaten earth, reinforced with clay and roofed with nylon fabric. These constructions are raised off the ground to keep out the damp.[9] One bold builder even located his beaten earth home on the beach, protected by sandbag barriers. Others try to work with the clay they have to hand, using traditional artisanal techniques to start a brickworks. These are only some

INGENUITY

examples among many of Palestinian ingenuity in the face of their endless ordeal. Unusable solar panels are recycled into water purifiers; with a bit of cardboard and wax, an empty corned beef tin is transformed into a stove; children cut puppets from egg boxes; knitting needles are fashioned from bits of wood, while sewing machines are turned by bicycle wheels.

But we should be careful not to idealise this everyday resistance by the powerless. The women and men of Gaza are worn out by having to rebuild what has been erased so many times. In March 2022 I visited Samir Mansour at the bookshop and publishing house he had reopened in the centre of Gaza City, after the Israelis had bombed his previous shop ten months before. It was a lively place that was always full, not so much with customers as with anonymous punters soothed by this oasis of books. The son of a bookseller himself, in October 2023 Mansour had to cope with the destruction of his new bookshop. Now his one dream is that he and his family will come through the conflict intact. Although in December 2024, when he received the Prix Voltaire of the International Publishers Association, he expressed his intention to "continue to publish and print", his heart is no longer in it.[10]

At the same time Mahmoud Assaf, author of many essays, is wondering what to do with his life's work, a collection of thirty thousand books that he has assembled in his Gaza home. It's being damaged by the hostilities while Assaf has spent his savings seeking refuge with his family, first in Khan Younis and then in Rafah, before they found themselves in a tent in Deir al-Balah. A baker who had run out of fuel offered to buy all his books to burn, arguing that by selling them he would be helping to "feed his people". But Assaf could not agree to this sacrifice, because "to survive by turning knowledge into ashes tastes of death".[11] To date his invaluable collection has not yet been cast into the flames.

SMOKE

THE MEN AND WOMEN of Gaza have always enjoyed smoking, for the latter the odd hookah with the girls, for the former a cigarette pulled from their daily packet of twenty. After taking control of the Strip by force in June 2007, Hamas was tempted to ban tobacco. Frustrated that they could not fight the "Zionist enemy" other than in cycles of clashes that remained fairly brief, if disastrous for civilians, they turned their militant aggression on their own population, whom they ordered to comply with their vision of a supposed "moral order". At that time I calculated Gaza to be the territory most densely controlled by so-called "security" forces—in reality political police—in an Arab world already saturated with and constrained by political police of the same ilk.

This pressure from the police and militia simply added to Gaza's "nightmare within the nightmare" of Hamas domination under the Israeli blockade. The most virulent fundamentalists unearthed mediaeval fatwas to justify the prohibition of tobacco, on the grounds that it causes "intoxication" similar to that of alcohol and equally reprehensible. Yet the theological debate had been settled back in the Ottoman Empire of the seventeenth century, judging as licit both tobacco and its taxation by the Islamic rulers of the day.[1] Faced with uproar from Gazans, Hamas came to the same conclusion and decided to tolerate tobacco and to tax it accordingly. Meanwhile alcohol remained strictly prohibited, even in private spaces, and Islamist militiamen did not hesitate to burst into gatherings of friends or families at the slightest suspicion.

As well as obtaining considerable revenue from taxing tobacco, Gaza's Islamist masters also engaged in the highly profitable business of smuggling it in from Egypt. However, the most important thing for the militants remained their control over Gaza's main source of addiction—a third of the male population are smokers. The IDF were aware of this dependency and, in October 2023, imposed an embargo on cigarettes that no one could describe as "humanitarian". In Gaza rumour had it that this unprecedented embargo was intended to "make Gazans more nervous and the security chaos worse".[2]

Egypt and Israel authorised half a dozen large merchants to bring in commercial convoys through the Rafah crossing. Although some were involved in cigarette smuggling, which the embargo made particularly profitable, the number of packets coming into Gaza each month fell from around 12 million to only 2 million.[3] The smugglers also stockpiled their wares to make the shortage worse and maximise their profits. Prices rose to a thousand shekels—more than $300—for a packet of cigarettes or a kilo of raw tobacco, known as "Arab tobacco". Cigarette papers went from 1 to 100 shekels a packet, as did even the prices of tea leaves, jute leaves and roselle petals, which were mixed with tobacco or smoked instead. One cigarette would now be shared between three or four smokers, and on social media you would find offers to exchange half a cigarette for a little hookah tobacco.

The Israeli offensive against Rafah on 6 May 2024 led to the closure of the Egyptian border, forcing cigarette smugglers to turn to the humanitarian convoys. They would entice the drivers with bribes or, where that proved impossible, find a way to hide their goods in previously identified trucks, which then became a target for rival gangs seeking to seize the loot for their own advantage.[4] The IDF was not always hostile to the smuggling, which offered it yet another way to discredit the international organisations. At any rate, it had privatised the direct management of Kerem Shalom, handing it over to security firm Sheleg Lavan, which worked for a limited number of hours per day.

Cigarettes became so highly prized that they sold only singly, at 90 shekels a piece in mid-June 2024 and 120 two weeks later. The benchmark brand on this informal market was the Egyptian Karelia, with even more exorbitant prices for authentic Marlboros. But war profiteers were not the only ones to exploit the withdrawal symptoms of Gaza's smokers. Rather than dropping its usual evacuation orders, on 9 August Israeli planes dropped cigarettes on Khan Younis, where a new offensive was under way. Each cigarette came with the message: "Hamas is burning Gaza. Want more? Call this number." The luckiest ones picked up a whole packet, bearing the message, "Tobacco is dangerous to health, but Hamas is worse" with a picture of Sinwar with two satanic horns.[5]

In that summer of scarcity Karelia prices went up and up and even reached 200 shekels in the autumn. In late 2024, despite flashy signs promoting "The Hookah Kings" or the famous portrait of Che Guevara with a Havana cigar, the "cigarette sellers" whose stalls I saw were offering only adulterated refills for vapes. But I did hear of family quarrels aggravated by lack of nicotine, husbands made brutal by withdrawal, wives accusing their spouses of spending the family budget on a handful of cigarettes, and households torn apart by the shameful theft of a precious packet. Meanwhile the Islamist militia meted out the same cruel punishments, kneecapping cigarette smugglers and roadside bandits alike.

Diehard smokers give me impassioned descriptions of the different varieties of "Arab tobacco" rolled by sellers along the coast road. Chami is produced locally for the most part, on tobacco parcels cultivated east of Deir al-Balah. Deifa is said to be from the West Bank, although it is generally cut with Egyptian tobacco. Ersatz versions full of fig leaves or guava leaves are regarded with scorn. There is talk of the lost paradise of hookahs by the sea, evenings perfumed with coffee and tobacco, the days when you counted in packets rather than cigarettes— let alone drags. And we listen in silence to the chants of Umm Kulthum, because night has fallen and the "Star of the Orient", as the Egyptian diva is known, has risen with the moon.

Yet, in the early days of 2025 I sense a livelier tone in the chat about tobacco prices, which every smoker can tell you in detail without a moment's thought. It's hard to believe, but you can now buy a Karelia for just 150 shekels. When the price drops to 100 shekels, eyes shine with a light that seemed to have gone out forever; cigarettes saved for great occasions are taken out and enjoyed because people at last believe they will soon be followed by many more. The trend is confirmed. The profiteers dump their stock and the Karelia drops to 80, then 60, 50, then 40 shekels. And Gazans start madly hoping again, because the one thing that can make the smugglers loosen their grip, the one and only thing, is an end to the siege and the hostilities.

WAITING

GAZANS KNOW THE WORLD has abandoned them. At first they believed that images of the slaughter would so horrify the international public that they would demand action to end it. The realisation that this was not going to happen compounded the wounds of the injured with its own pain. People cursed the Arab regimes for their passivity, and even complicity. Little was expected of the European countries, which sent no representatives demanding to be let into Gaza. As for the United Nations, their presence and help were appreciated, with little distinction made between the various agencies and their respective missions. However, it was obvious that international organisations were vulnerable to the diktats of the occupiers, even without knowing the details of the incident on 5 January 2025, when a World Food Programme convoy was hit by sixteen bullets near the entrance of the Netzarim Corridor.[1]

Yet the word "truce" is on the lips of every man, woman and child. They are lucid when it comes to the difference between a suspension of hostilities—a simple truce—and a proper ceasefire preparing the way for a lasting agreement on Gaza's future. But they still long for a truce, however temporary. They long for it with all of their exhausted bodies and grieving souls. Here again, there is no room for illusions as to who might decide life and death in Gaza. An old man with a deeply lined face, resting on crutches and his one leg, speaks of a truce "God willing—and Netanyahu". His family gathered around him, from youngest to eldest, nod in silence, while the dull thud of an artillery shell landing a few hundred metres away elicits no reaction.

A HISTORIAN IN GAZA

Gazans understand that their fate is in the hands of one man, the only one to whose will the Israeli prime minister will bow, a man still asleep when their day is already well advanced, a man who calls press conferences while they are asleep, a man who will fuel the invaders' war machine until he decides too much is too much. This man, the most powerful on the planet, now has two faces: that of the current tenant of the White House and that of his predecessor, who is now also his successor. Gaza spits in the departing face of Joe Biden, who made so many promises he didn't keep. Today Gaza projects its dreams onto the grumpy face of Donald Trump. Who cares that he threatens "hell" if the Israeli hostages are not freed?[2] Everyday life in Gaza is already hell, so any change would be better than enduring this endless asphyxiation.

The atmosphere in Gaza began to change on 9 January 2025, against a background of diplomatic ballet in Qatar, ferment on social media and carefully managed leaks in the Israeli and Arab press. Even increased bombardment, including of the "humanitarian zone", was endured with a fatality intended to be positive. Hadn't the same thing happened in all the previous conflicts—one last slaughter before the guns fell silent? And then doubt creeps in, because this war is not like the others, it has broken the bounds of every scenario of suffering. So people turn to foreigners, asking them earnestly, believing they're the ones who know. One has to respond kindly to these raw, suffering questioners, without, however, giving them false hope.

It's the children of Gaza who set the new tone with chants of "truce!", "truce!", "truce!", from one tent to the next, shouting "Stop the war!" at passing UN vehicles. On 10 January 2025, fuel shortages are still making Gaza stagger. Its hospitals are on the verge of breakdown, and now there are threats to telecommunications links, the one remaining window on the world. Having ravaged the north of the enclave, Israeli troops are now camped just outside Gaza City, which is within range of their tanks. On 11 January the bombardment of a school sheltering refugees in Jabaliya kills eight people. Meanwhile the area south of the "humanitarian zone" echoes to the pounding of anything still standing in Rafah. The artillery fire fills the sky with the white dust of destroyed buildings, with the occasional counterpoint of an airstrike and dark cloud from the eliminated target.

Despite these congested horizons, discussions abound on the agreement being sketched out in Doha. There's little interest in the details of the exchange of Israeli hostages and Palestinian prisoners. The focus is on how the Israelis might disengage, even though this would not happen until a second phase. People convince themselves that they will soon be able to go back up north and, if they find their houses destroyed, so what, they will plant their tents in the ruins. Anything rather than vegetate endlessly in the destitution of the "humanitarian zone". Swept along by enthusiasm, they believe the rumours that international forces are to be deployed in Gaza—who cares whether they're sent by Arabs, Europeans or the UN—because no one wants to imagine emerging from this nightmare only to fall back under the yoke of Hamas. And when they've used up all their arguments, they slam down their trump card: a Karelia is now only 30 shekels and the smugglers know more than we do, since they get fat at our expense.

Joe Biden's National Security Advisor said, "We are very, very close to a hostage deal", adding that "being close still means we are far because until you actually get across the finish line, we're not there".[3] Such sporting metaphors are incomprehensible to Gazans, who are now as sapped by hope as they long were by despair. How can they grasp that these ongoing negotiations are taking place within a framework that the White House set in place the previous spring? Luckily, they've forgotten the widespread joy of 6 May 2024, when a ceasefire was announced a few hours before Netanyahu decided to launch his offensive on Rafah.

The streets of Deir al-Balah are at fever pitch; altercations break out over trifling matters, at water points insults are hurled, and the slightest traffic jam threatens to degenerate into something much worse. Chattering children spread a false alarm like a powder trail from one end of the "humanitarian zone" to the other, triggering ululations and celebrations, before the sad reality reinstates itself. The sinister round of Israeli airstrikes goes on, with at least eighty killed on 13 and 14 January 2025, five of them in a school in central Gaza and four in tents north of Deir al-Balah.[4] The sound of bombardments hitting Khan Younis, to the east, and Rafah in the south echoes at regular intervals in Al-Mawasi, keeping the "humanitarian zone" residents on tenterhooks.

The day of 15 January 2025 extends in an ever more painful wait; everyone is glued to the news coming in dribs and drabs from Qatar, Israel and the United States, where Gaza's fate will be decided, far, far away from the Gazans themselves. While most of the displaced dream of returning home, others wish simply to give their dead a decent burial. All are longing for respite, rest, a proper shower, a night lit by electric light— simply a normal life at last.[5] While one swears to take advantage of the first partial opening of the Egyptian border, another only hopes for a little quiet in which to shed the tears held back so long. Meanwhile, yet another displaced person smiles for a humorous selfie on social media, showing him lying in the tent he vows to destroy as soon as a ceasefire is announced.

By nightfall, the tension that has been building since dawn is ready to explode. As soon as a few anonymous "official" sources announce an agreement, a joyful ovation rises up to the sky, punctuated by celebratory gunfire. It's only much later that the head of the Qatari government announces a prisoner exchange agreement between Israel and Hamas, followed by a "return to a lasting calm", with a view to a permanent ceasefire.[6] The distinction between these three phases and the guarantees from the United States, Qatar and Egypt have no importance for Gazans, intoxicated by what they believe is the end of the nightmare.

Doctors are carried like heroes at hospital doors. A journalist takes off his press vest and throws it on the ground, swearing he'll never need it again. There's drumming and lusty singing, people embrace with a new fervour, wishing each other peace, peace and more peace. Yet this night of celebration too brings mourning, with the deaths of at least forty people in Israeli bombardments. And Hamas militiamen parade briefly in a street in Khan Younis, ready to clamp the trap shut on Gaza as soon as it has been slightly opened.

On 16 January Gazans wake with heavy heads and weary smiles. They thought they'd been released, now they realise they are just relieved. They had celebrated an agreement only to find that nothing has been settled. Netanyahu has postponed his government's approval of the text to the next day. The Egyptian and Qatari mediators act impatient while the United States says nothing. The Qassam Brigades accuse the IDF of having put a hostage's life in danger with their strikes. The blackmail continues, and with it the bombardments, making this the deadliest day of the year so far. The International Federation for Human Rights describes as "cold-blooded murder" the Israeli strike on Gaza City that killed a humanitarian worker from its local branch, Ihab Faisal, along with his wife and their two daughters.[7]

On the morning of 17 January 2025 refugees from Deir al-Balah dig feverishly for anything that can be saved from a crater in the middle of their encampment, caused by a strike the night before.

A HISTORIAN IN GAZA

Witnesses say that the Israeli military is starting to dismantle part of its roadblock on the coast, at the end of the Netzarim Corridor. Although this is only a loosening at the margins, it does make a dent in the symbol of the division of Gaza into north and south. The news spreads, and with it the hope that the truce will soon come into force. Fishermen mend their nets among the tents so they can be ready when the sea is once more opened to their boats. And not only has the Karelia dropped to 15 shekels per cigarette, the price of a 25-kilo sack of flour, which reached thousands of shekels at its scarcest, has fallen in a few days from 400 to 80 shekels.

The wind turns for good. A United Nations convoy is allowed in at the Kerem Shalom crossing and travels through the hunting grounds of Abu Shabab's gang without incident. Although it is protected by Palestinian employees of the Egyptian security firm Al-Aqsa, the bandits have clearly spared the aid trucks. Looters even go one by one to express their remorse to Hamas, which grants them a public pardon, hoping that this magnanimity will impel the gangs to disband. As the sun sets over the coast road, joy ferments in the makeshift encampments. Smiling more fully than the day before, people tell each other, "We'll soon be home!" and "We're going back home!"

Shortly after midnight on 18 January 2025 Netanyahu's government finally approved the agreement that had already been signed by its representatives in Qatar. Psychodramas of this kind, where an extremist minority keeps the country in suspense, are a regular feature of Israeli democracy. Finance Minister Bezalel Smotrich was campaigning for the resettlement of Gaza and refused to go further than the truce brought by the first phase of the agreement, even if it meant sacrificing the hostages that had not yet been freed. He remained in his government post, unlike the other supremacist minister Itamar Ben Gvir, who resigned noisily, but without compromising the parliamentary majority. Meanwhile Netanyahu made use of these troublemakers to highlight his own very relative moderation.

The bombardments continued at the same pace, including on the "humanitarian zone", with five members of the same family, both parents and their three children, killed in a strike on a tent in Al-Mawasi. Although people knew that the risk went up with an approaching truce, they were still stunned when an F-16 dropped a bomb less than a kilometre to the south, in mid-morning, raising a dark cloud of smoke. Meanwhile, Israeli planes dropped leaflets on Nuseirat, showing a drawing of a family in the ruins and captioned in Arabic: "Another victory for the resistance?" Anything was worth trying to counter the triumphalist press releases from Hamas and its armed wing. This propaganda clash made little impression on ordinary Gazans, who were focused on the few hours still to survive before the start of the truce.

The atmosphere in Gaza City at that time was described by twenty-three-year-old journalist Hossam Shabat, injured two months before in an Israeli bombardment: "Time is no longer measured in minutes, but in whole lives of pain and tears. Every moment that passes heightens the fear and tension of those who wonder if they will survive long enough to see the ceasefire."[8] Israeli airstrikes continued to bring death and mourning to different sites in Gaza. To the south of the "humanitarian zone", the rumour of an Israeli withdrawal from Rafah in the late afternoon led groups of young people to try to sneak in. They were immediately met and pushed back by Israeli artillery, tanks and drones in a clatter of gunfire intercut with explosions, which became more intense as the sun went down and continued here and there in the distance throughout the night.

When dawn broke on 19 January 2025, Gazans held their breath. There were only two more hours before 8:30, when the truce was due to start. At the same time *Le Monde* published my piece on the shocking fragility of the agreement that had been announced four days earlier in Qatar and was supposedly about to come into effect.[9] For this much-touted accord was really just a practical calendar for the implementation of an earlier agreement announced by Joe Biden on 31 May 2024, and then ignored. It provided for three phases each lasting forty-two days, the first involving the freeing of thirty-three Israeli hostages, the second the release of the other surviving hostages and the third the return of bodies. The terms of the exchanges with Palestinians held in detention by Israel were the subject of bitter negotiations and varied according to whether the hostage was male or female, young or old, sick or injured, civilian or soldier. Other aspects of the agreement, such as the Israeli withdrawal, the return of the displaced population and humanitarian aid, were far less clear.

If the White House had managed to persuade Israel and coerce Hamas seven and a half months previously, it would have saved the lives of around 10,000 Palestinians and many Israeli hostages.[10] Biden and his administration bear a heavy responsibility for the continuation of this tragedy, through their repeated veto on a call for a ceasefire by the UN Security Council. The United States insisted that nothing must "compromise" their own mediation, even though it was constantly hindered by the cynicism of Netanyahu and Hamas. After the October 2024 killing of its leader Yahya Sinwar, Hamas was led in Gaza by his brother Mohammed, a hardened fighter with no political baggage who was prepared to sacrifice thousands of civilians in the name of "victory" over "the Zionist enemy".[11] Meanwhile, for the Israeli prime minister, this freewheeling war is the safest way for him to ensure he remains immune to the Israeli justice system, even if it meant getting rid of his Defence Minister in November 2024.

WAITING

In the early hours of 19 January 2025 sporadic gunfire and shelling were still shattering the winter quiet, without bothering the cockerels, dogs and donkeys that know nothing of human wars. Then, around 8 am, a dull hubbub arose and began to swell in the tents and alleyways. It grew louder and louder until, when the time came, it burst into shouts of joy, a cacophony of car horns and celebratory gunfire. But this joy was quickly extinguished. The IDF refused to agree to the implementation of the ceasefire until Hamas gave it the names of the three women to be freed that day. The Islamists claimed that there were just a few "technical" problems, while hooded militiamen brandishing Kalashnikovs once again paraded in Khan Younis. The terrifying dance of the F-16s began again in the Gaza sky as everyone gritted their teeth in fear of a new conflagration.

It was not until 9:30 that Hamas published the identities and photographs of the three Israeli hostages, 11 before Israel confirmed it had received them and 11:15 when the truce officially came into force. At least nineteen people were killed in Israeli bombardments during this delay: nine in Gaza City, six in Khan Younis, three in the north of Gaza and one in Rafah. One of the strikes killed Ahmed Al-Qidra and two of his children as he was transporting them east of Khan Younis on his donkey cart in the belief that the fighting had stopped.[12] These deaths were in addition to the 122 Palestinians already killed since the agreement was announced on the evening of 15 January. So this truce had a bitter taste of ashes. It did not stop Gazans up and down the Strip from at last expressing their relief. But their first thoughts went to the innumerable ghosts that will long haunt the territory, where thousands of bodies still lie buried in rubble.

TRUCE

WITH THE SUSPENSION OF hostilities in the late morning of 19 January 2025 huge numbers of displaced people decided to return as quickly as possible to what had been their homes. But at this stage the only routes open ran from Gaza City to Beit Hanoun in the north and from Khan Younis to Rafah in the south. The IDF warned that it would shoot anyone approaching the Netzarim Corridor, effectively prohibiting any movement of people between the north and south of the Gaza Strip. According to the calendar of the truce agreement, civilians had to wait until 25 January to travel from the "humanitarian zone" to Gaza City via the coast road.

On the first day of the truce, long lines of men, women and children leave the "humanitarian zone" on foot for Rafah. They have so longed for this moment that the distance no longer matters. The most prescient have booked a heavily loaded cart or even a tuk-tuk groaning with passengers, and there are also a very few cars and, already, ambulances. Israeli soldiers used live fire to greet those who ventured forth before the truce was officially proclaimed, while the ruins conceal their lethal share of unexploded munitions.

For what the first to arrive discover is indeed a landscape of ruins. They knew it would be, of course, but the reality still comes as a shock. They dig through the rubble, trying to rescue a stove, tools and clothes miraculously preserved—crumbs of their former lives. The parents of Ayah Al-Dabba, a teenage girl shot dead by Israeli troops in May 2024 and hurriedly buried where she lay, discover to their horror that her remains have been exhumed and scattered. An old man fills his mouth with Rafah earth and a young man fills his lungs with Rafah air: "the sweetest in the world".

These scenes of returning to ruins are repeated in the north of Gaza. People comfort themselves with the thought that they have survived, staggering in the face of so much devastation, and pause to contemplate the remains of a building under which someone close, or many close to them, remain buried. Sometimes there's a burst of relief at the discovery of a house that's still standing, and people congratulate themselves for taking the first opportunity to come and protect whatever's left from potential looters. Some plant a Palestinian flag on a heap of rubble, others wave it high to show that they're still here, standing proud, where the world should never have left them to suffer so long. In the face of so much loss and mourning, the psychologists fear a massive wave of collective decompensation when civilians suddenly lose the energy given them by the will to survive the ongoing hostilities.

Rami Abou Jamous, three-times winner of the Prix Bayeux for war correspondents in 2024, conveys the popular sentiment with a stubborn smile and simple words. Holding his son in his arms outside the family tent, he films this moment of "small joy, tinged with a lot of sadness", when the depth of loss risks "reopening wounds" instead of "bandaging" them: "We will rebuild, but we have to start by rebuilding the person, the man, the child, then we will rebuild Gaza. We are optimists, we will do all that we can to get Gaza and Palestine going again, we'll be like phoenixes, we will rise from under the rubble and we will rebuild again."

The red fire engines and the civil defence ambulances are the first to pass by in procession, cheered by this population that owes them so much. Journalists form a circle to take off their bulletproof vests and throw them on the ground, jointly repeating the gesture of a single bold colleague on the evening of 15 January 2025. And each doctor, photographer and stretcher-bearer remembers a fallen comrade, a dead colleague, silently weeping for their absence and praying that their soul will rest in peace. Health professionals and press are feted everywhere as the real heroes of this hell that has lasted over fifteen months.

The Islamists, who had kept their heads down for fear of Israeli strikes, manoeuvre to take advantage of the popular joy. Their Minister of the Interior announces that Hamas units will be deployed across the enclave. Police in blue uniforms appear at the crossroads of Deir al-Balah, clearing the makeshift stalls to ease the flow of traffic and, crucially, to mark the return of their "order". The parades of the Qassam Brigades' hooded militiamen are more choreographed, with signs to the glory of Hamas handed out in advance to children along the route. Videographers are pre-positioned to immortalise this moment of celebration for the men who went underground while their compatriots were being massacred.

This theatre reached the heights of propaganda on the afternoon of 19 January 2025, when a Hamas convoy in central Gaza drove to meet the vehicles from the International Committee of the Red Cross (ICRC) tasked with taking the three freed hostages to Israel. The handover took place in a small square chosen by Hamas to maintain the illusion of a dense crowd. The hooded escorts in impeccably belted combat dress sported Kalashnikovs pointed at the sky and the badge of the Nukhba, the Hamas shock troops that had spearheaded the bloodbath of 7 October 2023. With the cameras watching, their commander signed the document for the handover of the young women, who disappeared into an ICRC bulletproof car after receiving an "end of captivity" certificate from their jailers.

This impeccably staged scene, widely seen throughout the world, was intended to show that Hamas and its so-called "elite units" had lost none of their operational capability and discipline. The sleight of hand would have been easily uncovered if the international press had been able to attend. But they seem to have got used to following events in Gaza at a distance, through phones and screens, becoming the dupe of many a manoeuvre. The IDF, which had recently organised a visit to Jabaliya for a handful of western reporters travelling in its armoured vehicles, continued to deny foreign journalists free access to Gaza. So what Gazan would dare express their rancour against Hamas and its militia, who had reappeared with their weapons and arrogance intact? Who would dare point to their responsibility in the unspeakable disaster, now that their menacing shadow was already omnipresent?

Once again, although Netanyahu's government and Hamas leaders were engaged in a ruthless war, their interests coincided to distort reality in Gaza. This cynical convergence was simply the fruit of diplomacy that claims to be transactional, while trampling on both diplomatic principles and humanitarian law. The United States used their veto four times, in October and December 2023 and again in February and November 2024, to prevent the UN Security Council calling for an immediate ceasefire and the unconditional release of the Israeli hostages. They allowed Netanyahu's government to conduct an extraordinarily vicious campaign against the UN, which it regularly accuses of being "antisemitic", while the Israeli parliament voted to ban UNRWA, the UN agency for Palestinian refugees.

Trump's "art of the deal" continued Biden's demolition of international law, carried out piecemeal over the fifteen months of Israel's war against Gaza, rather than Hamas. Ignorance of, and indeed scorn for local realities, whether human, political or simply logistical, made this agreement unstable even before it came into force. Its three guarantors held press briefings dripping with smugness in Washington, Doha and Cairo, although none of them had a representative in Gaza to monitor the implementation of the agreement. The tripartite structure also enabled each guarantor to absolve itself of responsibility for any potential crisis by blaming the other two.

An agreement worthy of the name would have needed far more solid guarantees and, crucially, an oversight mechanism on the ground, with sanctions for any violation. But there was none of that, since the fate of Gaza and its population was seen only through the prism of an exchange of human beings, a vision shared by Netanyahu's government and the Hamas leadership. The humanitarian aid so desperately awaited by over two million civilians in Gaza is mentioned solely in the two concluding lines of the agreement of 15 January 2025, and in terms that are at best evasive: "Humanitarian aid procedures under the agreement will be done subject to the humanitarian protocol agreed upon under the supervision of the mediators." Over the following days the United States, Qatar and Egypt devoted all their energy to ensuring that the detainees were exchanged, rather than developing a "humanitarian protocol".

In the absence of such a protocol, on 19 January 2025 international aid had not been formally "agreed" by anyone. But the UN, which had been waiting for this opportunity since the start of the conflict, drove 630 trucks into Gaza on this first day of the truce. Half of them came into the north through the Zikim crossing, to supply Gaza City. This loosening of the Israeli restrictions was supposed to be lasting, as it allowed aid in at pre-war levels. It reached the target number, identified in vain by the White House back in May 2024, of 600 trucks per day, including 50 carrying fuel. And, miraculously, the looters had vanished, revealing that they were after all simply a component of the Israeli aggression against Gaza.

But the developing truce lifted more than fifteen months of siege imposed on Gaza only to re-establish the blockade in force over the sixteen previous years. The bit players in this imprisonment mechanism indicated their readiness to reprise their roles under the aegis of the United States with Israel's agreement. The Palestinian Authority in Ramallah claimed to be ready to help control the Rafah crossing with Egypt, where it previously had acted simply as a buffer force to avoid direct contact with Hamas. The European Union also offered its services in Rafah, while proposing to support medical evacuations to Egypt—another bit part.

The first night of the truce was serene for the people of Gaza, whom the more frequent sound of drones did not disturb, since it no longer augured potential bombardment. As part of the agreement the Israeli military had suspended their reconnaissance flights for ten hours per day, and indeed twelve hours when hostages were being freed. Perhaps to make up for this frustration, they increased the number of night flights. Not that this mattered to Gazans, who awoke on 20 January 2025 under a sky once again clear of the detested drones. Many of the coast road stalls stood open to the four winds, deserted by traders who had already returned to the ruins of Rafah. You'd see carts overloaded with mattresses, clothing, blankets and modest pieces of furniture, cars bursting with passengers, and tuk-tuks that spluttered by, but never stalled, all of them heading south.

On the second day of the truce, Gaza's civil defence force could take a little rest. These ambulance drivers and paramedics had been through an appalling ordeal, taking enormous risks to save thousands of their compatriots. Ninety-four of them were killed in the fifteen months of the conflict and nearly half had been injured.[1] However, this rest was merely respite as, despite the suspension of hostilities, people were still being killed by Israeli bullets for going too close to their lines to the south and east of Rafah. Some fifty bodies had been recovered from the ruins of Rafah the day before, and the number doubled in the course of this second day. The IDF had abandoned damaged armoured vehicles and teenagers climbed into one of them to siphon oil from the engine.

In Al-Mawasi the fruit and vegetable stalls emptied in the morning due to prices that, without returning to pre-war levels, had become reasonable. An egg that cost 4 shekels a week before was now worth only one. And a stallholder would even accept a 10-shekel coin, scrubbing it to pretend it was new. One falafel seller said he would be going back up the coast road to Jabaliya in five days' time, when the Netzarim roadblock was scheduled to open. But the advice was to send men in first as scouts, before exposing the family in the middle of the ruins and far from any water point. The Hamas police were still deployed at crossroads and patrolling here and there, while the hooded militiamen of the Qassam Brigades kept a lower profile after their demonstration of strength the day before.

Ten thousand kilometres and seven time zones from Gaza, Trump was noisily taking credit for the success of the truce, seeing it as a direct consequence of his choice of "peace through strength", a phrase he repeated in capital letters on social media. He had just given a speech to ecstatic supporters vowing to "stop the chaos in the Middle East" and "avoid a third world war".[2] But as soon as he entered the White House, the new president tempered this optimism by comparing Gaza to a "demolition site" and saying he was "not sure" that the truce would hold: "It's not our war, it's their war. But I'm not confident."[3]

A HISTORIAN IN GAZA

The doubts expressed by the most powerful man in the world did not seem to affect the UN officials in charge of the convoy in which, on the morning of 21 January 2025, my departure from the Gaza Strip had been "coordinated". I had not received the indispensable green light from COGAT until the evening before, as the unwritten rule requires. I learned immediately afterwards that, due to the truce, the UN had decided to "test" a new arrangement with serious security implications. Until that point the UN had transported all "coordinated" persons in its armoured vehicles, which it had now decided to reserve for its own staff, leaving NGOs to join the convoy in their own unprotected cars.

The assembly point in Khan Younis was an UNRWA centre that had been one of the UN's busiest sites in the Gaza Strip. The Palestinian staff were now worried that they would soon be laid off due to Israel's ban on UNRWA's activities. While those responsible for the convoy recognised that the situation was "very volatile", they expressed faith in Israeli guarantees that we would all reach Kerem Shalom unhindered. But they clearly did not believe their own words since, instead of having one of their armoured vehicles accompany or bring up the rear of the convoy, they placed all five of their bulletproof cars at the front, with only a radio link to the fifteen or so other vehicles. In practice this was no longer one connected convoy, but an amalgamation of convoys, which the UN had ensured it could exit in its protected vehicles should an incident occur.

The procession set off through the dusty streets of Khan Younis. On the left was the town's central prison, from which the prisoners had escaped at the start of the hostilities. Its walls had been damaged but not destroyed by Israeli strikes, leading large numbers of displaced people to seek refuge inside. To the right a huge sewage tank lay open to the sky, its smell kept bearable by the winter temperatures. Opposite, what was once a main road with arcades was now no more than a series of bombed-out buildings. Graffiti proclaimed that this devastated zone was still the fiefdom of the al-Astal family, perhaps the most powerful in Khan Younis. After crossing the city west to east we turned south down the Salah al-Din Road. The traffic was denser, making it hard for the convoy to stay together, though the tuk-tuks and carts did move aside to let the bothersome procession pass, accompanying their manoeuvres with eloquent hand gestures. Even the hooded militiamen armed with assault rifles at the roadblocks took no interest in the convoy, instead stopping and searching their compatriots' cars at random. This was how the Qassam Brigades asserted their control over at least part of this strategic road, leaving the Hamas police to cover what was left of the cities.

At the Shoka roundabout the convoy forked southeast, crossing Rafah's field of ruins. We were now entering the hunting grounds of Abu Shabab's gang, used by the IDF as a buffer against the Islamist fighters. But the days of looting were past, since the truce was allowing humanitarian aid trucks in once more. Journalists had set up cameras on tripods to film the arrival of this international manna. All around there was nothing but collapse and desolation. Nevertheless, a family had pitched their tent on a square of rubble, lighting up its greyness with their garishly coloured blankets. Another had taken refuge next to two walls that met at a right angle, providing a little shade and, who knows, maybe comfort.

Nothing caught my eye in this sea of rubble until we approached the concrete wall of the border with Egypt. I recognised the tongue of Israeli asphalt down which I'd entered Gaza by night, a little over a month before, walking in the headlights of the military jeeps. That night the UN security staff had already "tested" a procedure so hazardous that it was immediately dropped. The arrangement used on 21 January 2025 would similarly not be repeated, the next convoy being cancelled following exchanges of fire. It was only later that I could admit to fearing the worst during this journey. For now, I focused on getting through the border controls at Kerem Shalom without a hitch. The due presence of my name on a list opened the exit gates from the Gaza Strip. I still had to wait for a police escort to accompany our Israeli bus to the Jordanian border. But I was already engrossed in the works of Stendhal: "Believe nothing, my friend, but what you have seen and you will be all the wiser".[4]

ONE-FIFTH

DESPITE THE INTENSITY OF my thirty-two days and thirty-three nights in the Gaza Strip, I am well aware of the limitations of my experience. I was always dry, if not warm, even when it was pelting with rain. My meals were guaranteed and I always had drinking water to hand. I could sleep soundly, within the regulatory protection of a wall inside a wall, even amid the flares and sounds of bombardments and automatic gunfire. I was always secure in my privilege—the most precious you can have in Gaza—of being able to leave, albeit after a complicated process of "coordination", but with my head high and without fear for my family and property.

My restrictions were largely geographical. Aside from a return trip from Kerem Shalom to Khan Younis, out by night, back by day, I never left the invisible boundaries of the "humanitarian zone", which you cross at your own risk and peril. It's true that the Israeli bombardment did not spare this so-called "safe" zone, and noticeably increased in January 2025, averaging at least one strike per day until the truce.[1] I trembled when some of these strikes hit and I saw the damage they inflicted. But I did not suffer the fear aroused by evacuation orders or the panic of fleeing by night, which the "humanitarian zone" as a whole is spared. It's true that more than half of Gaza's population have been crammed into this spit of dry, inhospitable land. But although I moved around it in all directions, this enclave within the enclave remains no more than one-fifth of the total area of the Gaza Strip.

When I came in, I crossed Rafah only by night. Later, I saw mushroom clouds of smoke rising daily into the sky from Israeli shelling, just a few kilometres to the southeast, below Tal al-Sultan, or "Sultan's Hill". I had a clearer view of strikes on the no man's land of Shakush, the "Hammer" so close to the southern edge of the "humanitarian zone" that a burning fragment fell into it. I admired the sunset on the Egyptian border, but I saw nothing of the Philadelphi Corridor patrolled by Israeli armoured vehicles. I was permitted merely to travel past Rafah's appalling sea of ruins on the morning of my departure. Yet I did see Rafah in the intense eyes of those who had sworn to return because that is where their land is, where their home is.

 I didn't return to Gaza City, where my routine once took me from the street of three universities to the seafront cafés, the Pasha's Palace, the fishing port, the monument to the Unknown Soldier and the French Institute. I could do no more than comfort my friends distraught at the loss of their paradise, sharing their memories and stories as they poured out their pain and longing. I confess that I trembled at their tales of terror in the darkness, of frantic, breathless flight and Russian roulette at the Israeli roadblocks. But I saw nothing of the Netzarim Corridor, its blasted expanse of ruins that slices through the enclave from one side to the other, as though there were anything left to shatter or strip away. Yet I did see Gaza City in the intense eyes of those who had sworn to return because that is where their land is, where their home is.

 I did not return to Jabaliya, birthplace of the first intifada in 1987, which would push the peoples of Palestine and Israel down the path of peace six years later. I simply lost myself in aerial views of a devastation too methodical to have been caused by a simple earthquake. And I listened respectfully to the words of women and men who had been shot at again and again, not necessarily directly at them, but next to them, above their heads, so close, too close, inside their houses until they left them, on the road until they took it and didn't look back, driven, chased, pursued. But I saw nothing of the appalling destruction by diggers and bulldozers transformed into weapons of mass destruction. Yet I did see Jabaliya in the intense eyes of those who had sworn to return because that is where their land is, where their home is.

That this passionate desire to return should resonate so urgently in Gaza comes as no surprise to a historian. The Palestinians' refusal, in 1947, to allow the UN to establish a Jewish state on more than half of their land unleashed a war between Jews and Arabs, as appalling as any civil war, that saw waves of displaced people arrive in Gaza. These flows increased after the proclamation of the State of Israel in May 1948 and the deployment of Egyptian soldiers along the Mediterranean as far as Al-Majdal, north of Gaza. Though the newly formed IDF bombarded it from air, land and sea, the zone remained afloat as a "Noah's ark" for the disappearing Palestine, as told to me by refugees from that time. But the Egyptian battalions were overwhelmed at Al-Majdal and fell back to Beit Hanoun, while an Israeli attempt to encircle them drove the other units to the east of Gaza and Khan Younis. Capitulation was avoided only by keeping open the crossing from Rafah to the Sinai Peninsula.

The ceasefire agreed by Cairo in January 1949 drew the boundaries of a "Gaza Strip" under Egyptian administration, which thus avoided being absorbed into Israeli territory or annexed by the Jordanian monarchy. This was the Nakba or "catastrophe" for Palestine and the exodus of the majority of its people, who were forced, particularly in Gaza, to take shelter in tents and depend on international aid, initially from the American Quakers and the Turkish government. The uprooted farmers missed their land and it pained them that they could not feed themselves with the fruits of their labour. Some found their way into what was now enemy territory, leading to inexhaustible vendettas with the inhabitants of the border kibbutzim. Al-Majdal was Hebraised into Ashkelon, expelling its remaining core of Palestinian inhabitants southwards. The gates shut on the Gaza enclave, which had escaped the disaster and was now under surveillance on its northern border from the Israeli position at Erez, opposite Beit Hanoun.

Obviously, the Nakba of the past resonates in the Nakba of today. For Israelis, the bloodbath perpetrated by Hamas and its allies in October 2023 reawakened the fear of annihilation that gripped the Zionist partisans in the autumn of 1947, two and a half years after the liberation of the concentration camps. Netanyahu's government constantly escalates its actions and pounds its "red lines" in order to "restore deterrence" and gain "total victory" over Hamas. This is more about opportunism on the part of the Prime Minister than a clear, well-argued military strategy. It requires propaganda blinded by its own outrageous exaggerations to dare to invoke the "war of independence" of 1948–1949, when the newly proclaimed Jewish state had neither nuclear weapons nor unconditional US support.

The effects of the Gaza "catastrophe" in the winter of 2024–2025 are however much worse than those of the Palestinian Nakba of 1947–1948. This is incontestably true in relative terms, with 1 % of the Arab population of Palestine killed during the original Nakba (the same proportion as for the Jewish population) as opposed to 2.3 % of Gazans killed since October 2023. The absolute numbers are even more overwhelming, the first Arab–Israeli war having ended with some 750,000 Palestinian refugees, compared to the 1.9 million now displaced in the Gaza Strip. And although many more humanitarian organisations are much more active there than during the winter of 1947–1948, the international media, both then and now, are resigned to being based solely in Israeli territory.

Al-Majdal was no further from Gaza City then than Khan Younis is now. Yet Al-Majdal became Ashkelon, closed to its expelled inhabitants, who have since been confined in the former oasis that is now the Gaza "Strip". This traumatic experience of forced uprooting underpins the collective identity of Gazans, two-thirds of whom are refugees from 1948 or their descendants. The winter of 1948–1949 did not lead to a spring of return, but to another winter of exile, after which the UN built more permanent refugee camps. After 2023–2024's winter of fire and ash, no one wants to end a second winter in the tents of humiliation, for fear of finding themselves stuck there for ever. In Gaza every heart, song and wall speaks only of return.

The return began spontaneously, unbidden and unorganised, as soon as the truce was declared in the late morning of 19 January 2025. So I experienced in Gaza what I hoped, but did not really believe, would be the last month of the war, a month in which at least 1,407 Palestinians were killed and 3,753 injured. In that same month eleven journalists were killed, at least five of them deliberately. And Gaza's hospitals recorded the deaths of eight infants from hypothermia. Fewer than 100 patients benefitted from medical evacuation, when according to the WHO over 12,000 needed it urgently.[2] The evacuation orders from the IDF in that month applied to a total of one-sixth of the area of Gaza. Such excessive warnings could not fail to be massively ignored by their target population but enabled the aggressors to shrug off all responsibility.

Summarised here, in words and figures too raw not to be brutal, is what I experienced and saw all around me during that month and more in Gaza. Allow me to mention only with restraint the distress that was revealed to me, the hopes expressed and the flaws confessed, all marks of a trust that does me honour and by which I am bound. When the time came for goodbyes, with each I promised to return "for good" to the recovered home, the rebuilt house and to a Gaza finally at peace.

SAMSON

"A PALESTINIAN'S ONLY FRIEND is his donkey." How many times have I heard that bitter remark amid the devastation of Gaza. And it resonates sadly at a time when grandiose expressions of solidarity with Palestine by Arabs, Muslims, progressives and internationalists alike have proved tragically ineffective in the darkest of times. The Palestinians abandoned by all in Gaza have been able to count on none but their donkeys and carts to move their families and a few possessions from one refuge to the next, braving scarcities and bombardments. And these emaciated donkeys, as malnourished as their masters, have helped them more than all the international humanitarian law, endlessly violated with impunity in the sealed space of Gaza.

On 7 October 2023, Gaza and its people had already spent sixteen years blocked by three impasses: Israeli, Palestinian and humanitarian. The Israeli impasse stemmed and stems from Israel's refusal to consider Gaza otherwise than in the strict terms of Israeli security, with no care for the human reality of Gazans and their socio-political dynamics. This blindness, which is itself ethically debatable, did not spare Israel from the bloodiest day in its history. As for the sound and fury of "total victory" over Hamas, fifteen months of devastation later, this has merely led to the Islamists regaining control over the enclave. And with good reason: only a return to negotiations for a two-state solution can open up any real prospect of a future and establish a government in Gaza with enough legitimacy to replace Hamas and guarantee Israel's security.

A HISTORIAN IN GAZA

The Palestinian impasse stemmed and stems from its Israeli counterpart, and from the absolute priority given by the Palestinian factions to their own interests, with no care for the national rights or physical integrity of the Palestinian people. A tragedy on the scale of the modern Nakba that has shattered Gaza should have given rise to an unprecedented wave of national unity. Not only has it not done so, but Hamas chose to offer up hundreds of thousands of its compatriots to the inevitable reprisals of Israel while preserving an organisation robust enough to be deployed once the truce had been declared, while the Palestinian Authority, for fear of compromising its Ramallah fiefdom, has settled for providing potential security backup on the border between Gaza and Egypt.

The humanitarian impasse stemmed and stems from the other two, since there is no point in claiming to provide lasting help to a population deprived of any political prospects and subject, albeit remotely, to an occupier's diktats. Since 2007, colossal sums have been spent on keeping Gaza afloat, when the blockade forbade any development worthy of the name and the enclave was mercilessly ravaged by recurrent conflicts. The methodical destruction inflicted since October 2023, in addition to an unprecedented siege, has led to a humanitarian disaster that, to date, it has been possible only to contain, despite the considerable energy expended on avoiding the worst. This situation will continue as long as there is no end to Israel's physical blockade and political rejection of the two-state solution.

"Gaza is like a bizarre laboratory experiment, the aim of which is apparently to measure the resistance of two million guinea pigs living under a hermetically sealed bell jar".[1] Those are lines that I could have written, had they not already been penned seven years earlier by a French journalist reporting from Gaza. The observation remained the same, from one year to the next—

but worse, each time worse and worse still, until the absolute horror of the war that is still raging now. There's no merit in this lucidity, which is entirely apparent to anyone who goes to live among the "two million guinea pigs" under the "hermetically sealed bell jar", in the way I've described to you here.

No, nothing has changed under the Gaza sky, which will become truly open only when a road is opened towards a Palestinian state living in peace alongside Israel. What has changed from previous conflicts, which were comparatively limited in their duration and destruction, is that this time the ravages have been conducted systematically and methodically, week by week, month by month. What has changed is that this time our world could not pretend to be unaware of the scale of the disaster, and yet it has let it happen and sometimes applauded. This world—yours and mine—has simply not understood that what is happening in Gaza has and will have universal significance.

This is a world where Donald Trump can decide to turn the Gaza Strip into the "Riviera of the Middle East", even at the cost of expelling its population and forbidding their return. It's a world where the presidents of the European Commission and European Council have not opened their mouths to denounce such infamy. It's a world where the Israeli government can set up a special agency for the "voluntary departure" of the inhabitants of Gaza a few days before being invited to Brussels in the name of its "association" with the European Union.[2] This is a world where giving up is disguised as "realism" and low-grade schemers argue that, to preserve any potential US support for Ukraine, it's best not to bother too much about Gaza.

This is to forget that Trump's United States only has one ally, and that is Netanyahu's Israel. It's not the members of NATO and it's not Ukraine, whose resistance is a hindrance to the dream of a deal with Putin's Russia. Indeed, the US president chose his business and golf partner Steve Witkoff as his special envoy to both the Middle East and Russia. In between two audiences at the Kremlin, Witkoff encouraged Netanyahu to break the truce in Gaza by imposing a hermetic siege on 2 March 2025, with a return to massive bombardment two weeks later. Once again the evacuation orders rain down on an entirely defenceless population, while Israeli tanks hold Gaza in their vice once more, while strikes hit humanitarian workers and the western media remain banned from entry. It's the same horror, but worse every time.

Gaza's destruction has not only buried Gazan women, men and children. It has buried the norms of international law that were patiently constructed to ward off any repetition of the Second World War's barbarities. It has buried the diplomatic codes that, despite their rules and weaknesses, still served to calm disputes rather than make them worse. Gaza has now been handed over to the sorcerers' apprentices of deal-making, the AI gunners and the vultures who feed on human distress. It shows us the abjection of a world given up to the likes of Trump and Netanyahu, Putin and Hamas, a world that Gaza's abandonment has only brought closer.

This is why I decided to finish this book in Ukraine, where the prospect of such a world is no less dark than in Palestine. So I write about Gaza in Kyiv, as I wrote about Kyiv in Gaza, because no one people has fewer rights than any other, even if they are weaker—particularly if they are weaker. And not far from the university where I'm currently lecturing, a statue of Samson gives the Biblical figure his due honour. It does not celebrate "the vainglorious hero who let his own soul perish just to get even with the Philistines",[3] but is a Baroque "sculpture of Samson prising open the lion's mouth".[4] For this is the Samson with eyes wide open, who kills a lion with his bare hands, not the blind man who slaughters the Philistines and buries both them and himself.

Gaza, December 2024–Kyiv, March 2025

NOTES

NOTHING

1. Jean-Pierre Filiu, "Avoiding the Hamas trap in Gaza", *Le Monde*, 22 October 2023.
2. Jean-Pierre Filiu, "Destroying Hamas, or destroying Gaza", *Le Monde*, 17 December 2023.
3. Jean-Pierre Filiu, "How Israel is eliminating any alternative to Hamas in Gaza", *Le Monde*, 28 April 2024.

COORDINATION

1. The areas of East Jerusalem, the West Bank and the Gaza Strip are referred to in international law as "the Occupied Palestinian Territory", in the singular.
2. International Court of Justice, "Legal Consequences arising from the Policies and Practices of Israel in the Occupied Palestinian Territory, including East Jerusalem", The Hague, 19 July 2024, p. 33.
3. Press release from prime minister Ehud Olmert, Jerusalem, 19 September 2007.
4. Average based on 2,784 calories for men, 2,162 for women and 1,758 for children.
5. COGAT, "Food consumption in the Gaza Strip—Red lines", 1 and 27 January 2008, put online by the Israeli NGO Gisha, following a 5 September 2012 decision by the Israeli Supreme Court.

6. Paul Blumenthal, "Israeli president suggests that civilians in Gaza are legitimate targets", Politico, 17 October 2023.
7. Dr. Al-Balawi was not released until 5 January 2025, following repeated appeals from the World Health Organization and Jordan, of which he is a citizen.

THE ZONE

1. Out of the 1,028 airstrikes Israel carried out between 7 and 28 October 2023, 426 hit south of Wadi Gaza, although the population in the north was ordered to evacuated southward (Forensic architecture, "A spatial analysis of the Israeli military's conduct in Gaza since October 2023", 25 October 2024, p. 178).
2. United Nations Office for the Coordination of Humanitarian Affairs (OCHA), "Reported impact snapshot, Gaza", 29 October 2023.
3. The flour mill was destroyed on 15 November 2023. OCHA, "Hostilities in the Gaza Strip and Israel, Reported impact", 23 November 2023.
4. Forensic architecture, "A spatial analysis of the Israeli military's conduct in Gaza since October 2023", *op. cit.*, pp. 201 and 531.
5. This "corridor" bears the name of a religious settlement established there from 1972 until Israel's withdrawal in 2005.
6. An estimated 100,000 civilians have managed to flee to Egypt since October 2023, at the price of exorbitant fees paid to various intermediaries.
7. OCHA, "Humanitarian situation update 206, Gaza", 19 August 2024.
8. Benedict Garman and Richard Irvine-Brown, "Gaza 'humanitarian zone' struck almost 100 times since May, BBC Verify finds", BBC, 15 January 2025.
9. Refugees International, "Israel Fails to Comply with U.S. Humanitarian Access Demands in Gaza", 12 November 2024.
10. OCHA, "Reported impact snapshot, Gaza", 17 December 2024.
11. Médecins sans frontières (MSF), "Gaza, life in a deathtrap", 19 December 2024, p. 21.

THE PATRIARCH

1. Lucas Minisini, "The Holy Family Church, a precarious sanctuary

NOTES

for Gaza's Christians", *Le Monde*, 3 August 2024. This head-spinning proportion of 4 % of deaths due to the hostilities and deprivations, is consistent with the general proportion of direct and indirect victims of the conflict, each around 2 % of the population.
2. Agnès Pinard Legry, "François appelant chaque soir les chrétiens de Gaza", Aleteia, 23 January 2025.
3. "Malgré les protestations d'Israël, le pape condamne à nouveau "la cruauté" de la guerre à Gaza", *La Croix*, 22 December 2024.
4. Delphine Allaire, "Cardinal Pizzaballa aux chrétiens de Gaza: vous êtes la lumière de notre Église", *Vatican News*, 23 December 2024.
5. Lucas Minisini, "Gaza's 500 Christians celebrate second Christmas under bombs", *Le Monde*, 23 December 2024.

ONE NIGHT

1. The hospital was named for a prominent nationalist figure in Gaza, one of Yasser Arafat's brothers-in-arms assassinated by an Israeli commando squad in Beirut in 1973.
2. Message from Dr Hussam Abu Safiya, Beit Lahia, 23 December 2024.

CHRISTMAS

1. "Baby freezes to death in Gaza", *Time*, 25 December 2024.
2. "Four babies die of hypothermia in Gaza", CNN, 26 December 2024.
3. Rayhan Uddin, "Palestinian artist and husband killed in Israeli strike on Christmas Day", *Middle East Eye*, 25 December 2024.
4. Instagram @walaa.jom3a
5. "Dozens killed as Palestinians flee Israel's new offensive on Khan Younis", Al-Jazeera, 22 July 2024.

HOSPITALS

1. Briefing by Stéphanie Tremblay, Associate Spokesperson for the UN Secretary-General, New York, 23 December 2024.
2. Kaamil Ahmed, "Last major health facility in north Gaza 'out of service' after Israeli attack", *The Guardian*, 28 December 2024.
3. "Israel orders forced removal of Kamal Adwan's patients within 24 hours", *Middle East Eye*, 8 October 2024.

NOTES

4. Ruwaida Kamal Amer, "I will stay inside my hospital until the last moment", Electronic Intifada, 5 November 2024.
5. Fedaa Al-Qedra, "Injured Palestinian doctor remains relentless", Electronic Intifada, 23 December 2024.
6. "De premières informations font état de services-clés incendiés et détruits pendant le raid", WHO X account, 27 December 2024.
7. "Israel arrests hospital director in Northern Gaza", CNN, 28 December 2024.
8. Malak Tantesh and Julian Borger, "WHO 'appalled' by Israel attack on northern Gaza's last functioning major hospital", *The Guardian*, 28 December 2024.
9. Testimony from Rawiya Tamboura, 28 December 2024.
10. Testimony from nurse Shrouq Saleh to CNN, 27 December 2024.
11. "Israel arrests hospital director in Northern Gaza", *op. cit.*
12. Ahmed Dremly, "Israeli soldiers storm Gaza's Kamal Adwan hospital, force out semi-naked medics and patients", *Middle East Eye*, 28 December 2024.
13. Testimony given to Belal Mortaja, Gaza, 28 December 2024.
14. "Israel detains the director of one of Gaza's last functioning hospitals during a raid", CBS, 28 December 2024.
15. "Strapped down, blindfolded, held in diapers: Israeli whistleblowers detail abuse of Palestinians in shadowy detention center", CNN, 11 May 2024.
16. Louis Imbert, "Far right supporters storm Negev military detention center in Israel", *Le Monde*, 30 July 2024.
17. Al-Ahli was founded in 1882 by a local chapter of the Anglican church, but from 1954 to 1982 was administered by a Baptist mission, wherefore its nickname.
18. Mera Aladam, "Attacks on Gaza health sector make hospitals a 'battleground', WHO chief warns", *Middle East Eye*, 30 December 2024.
19. One example among many is an IDF statement on 27 December 2024 claiming that "Kamal Adwan serves a Hamas terrorist stronghold in northern Gaza, from which terrorists have been operating throughout the war".
20. United Nations Office of the High Commissioner for Human Rights,

"Attacks on hospitals during the escalation of hostilities in Gaza", 31 December 2024, p. 10.
21. *Ibid.*, p. 21.
22. Alexander Smith, "Information missteps have led to questions about Israel credibility", NBC, 18 November 2023.
23. Felicia Sideris and Caroline Quevrain, "Des otages à l'hôpital Al-Rantissi de Gaza? Les questions que pose la vidéo de l'armée israelienne", TF1, 15 November 2023.
24. Graeme Baker, "Israel Gaza: Hospitals caught on the frontline of war", BBC, 14 November 2024.
25. "L'hôpital Al-Shifa, centre de commandement du Hamas?", visual investigation by *Le Monde*, 3 December 2023.
26. Julian Borger, "IDF evidence so far falls well short of al-Shifa hospital being Hamas HQ", *The Guardian*, 17 November 2023.
27. Articles 18 and 19 of the fourth Geneva convention relative to the protection of civilian persons in time of war, 12 August 1949.
28. United Nations Office of the High Commissioner for Human Rights, "Attacks on hospitals during the escalation of hostilities in Gaza", 31 December 2024, pp. 12 and 13.
29. MSF, "Gaza, life in a deathtrap", 19 December 2024, p. 13.
30. *Ibid.*, p. 14.
31. Forensic architecture, "A spatial analysis of the Israeli military's conduct in Gaza since October 2023", 25 October 2024, p. 341.
32. "Emirati field hospital in Gaza conducts medical consultations via Starlink", WAM, 1 August 2024.
33. On 31 December 2024, 55 seriously injured people were able to leave the Palestinian enclave via Kerem Shalom and be flown from Eilat Airport to Abu Dhabi.
34. United Nations Office of the High Commissioner for Human Rights, "Attacks on hospitals...", *op. cit.*, p. 16.
35. *Ibid.*, p. 17.
36. *Ibid.*, p. 16.
37. ICC arrest warrants for Mr Netanyahu and Gallant, The Hague, 21 November 2024.
38. Healthcare Workers Watch, *The Killing, Detention and Torture of Healthcare Workers in Gaza*, 7 October 2024, p. 9.

39. MSF, "Gaza, life in a deathtrap", *op. cit.*, p. 17.
40. MSF, "Remembering our colleagues killed in Gaza", 21 March 2025.

WATER

1. Account related by Moaz Abou Tahaa, 31 December 2024.
2. Account related by Ashraf Abou Amra, 31 December 2024.
3. Account related by Nahed Hajjaj, 31 December 2024.
4. Gisha, "Still waters", 22 March 2022.
5. Human Rights Watch, "Extermination and acts of genocide", 19 December 2024, charts pp. 2 and 3.
6. *Ibid.*, p. 48.
7. *Ibid.*, p. 53.
8. *Ibid.*, p. 55.
9. OCHA, "Hostilities in the Gaza Strip and Israel", 24 January 2024.
10. Human Rights Watch, "Extermination and acts of genocide", *op. cit.*, p. 65.
11. *Ibid.*, p. 61.
12. OCHA, "Humanitarian situation update 212, Gaza", 2 September 2024.
13. These are laid out in the Wassenaar Agreement adopted in 1996, to which Israel is in fact not a party.
14. UNICEF, "Intensifying conflict, malnutrition and disease in the Gaza Strip creates a deadly cycle that threatens over 1.1 million children", 5 January 2024.
15. WHO, Health Cluster, "Occupied Palestinian territory: a year of crisis—health cluster overview", 17 October 2024.
16. WHO WASH Cluster and Health Cluster for the Occupied Palestinian Territory, "Urgent hygiene crisis: combatting diarrhea and skin infections in Gaza", 13 September 2024.
17. Leslie Roberts, "The virus that causes polio has been found in Gaza", *Science Insider*, 22 July 2024.
18. Jean-Philippe Rémy, "Gaza polio vaccination campaign has limited time and space to act", *Le Monde*, 11 September 2024.
19. 560,000 children received one dose of the vaccination as of 11 September 2024.
20. WHO news release, 23 October 2024.

NOTES

21. WHO news release, 1 November 2024.
22. OCHA, "Humanitarian situation update 251, Gaza", 31 December 2024.

AN ANNIVERSARY

1. Daniel Byman, "A war they are both losing", International Institute for Strategic Studies, 4 June 2024.
2. Ameneh Mehvar and Nasser Khdour, "After a year of war, Hamas is militarily weakened, but far from eliminated", ACLED, 6 October 2024.
3. See above, p. 37.
4. "IDF said it killed head of Southern Gaza Hamas' internal security apparatus", *Times of Israel*, 3 January 2025.
5. "Israeli airstrikes kill Gaza head of police, 67 others, Gaza authorities say", Reuters, Cairo, 2 January 2025.

WITNESSES

1. "Le journaliste Omar Dirawi, la prière des morts pour son frère, puis pour lui", Resalah, 4 January 2025.
2. Instagram @omar_aldirawi
3. "Israeli strike kills Palestinian journalist and his parents in Central Gaza", *Middle East Eye*, 3 January 2025.
4. "The journalists killed in Gaza, and what they tried to show the world", *Washington Post*, 9 February 2024.
5. Committee for the Protection of Journalists (CPJ), "Journalist casualties in the Israel-Gaza war", 3 January 2025.
6. Kathy Jones, "Israel-Gaza war brings 2023 journalist killing to devastating high", CPJ, 15 February 2024.
7. "Media freedom watchdog decries Israel's killing of journalists in Gaza", Al-Jazeera, 16 December 2024.
8. CPJ, "Father of Al-Jazeera's Anas al-Sharif killed in Gaza after journalist receives threats", 11 December 2023.
9. CPJ, "Journalist casualties...", *op. cit.*
10. RSF, "Palestine", in *World Press Freedom Index*, 3 May 2024.
11. Samuel Forey, "Rushdi Sarraj, Palestinian journalist and fixer, killed by Israeli strike in Gaza", *Le Monde*, 23 October 2023.

12. Piotr Smolar, "Dans la bande de Gaza, la marche du désespoir des Palestiniens", *Le Monde*, 31 March 2018.
13. Guillaume Gendron, "Gaza: un journaliste palestinien parmi les neuf tués de vendredi", *Libération*, 7 April 2018.
14. "Contradicting Israel, Journalists' Federation says slain Palestinian photographer was arrested and beaten by Hamas", *Haaretz*, 13 April 2018.
15. Forey, "Rushdi Sarraj", *op. cit.*
16. Samuel Forey, "En Palestine, la renaissance d'un cours d'eau après vingt ans d'efforts", *Le Monde*, 7 October 2023.
17. "The journalists killed in Gaza...", *op. cit.*
18. Christophe Ayad, "Enquête à Gaza: des vies en enfer", *Le Monde*, 8 September 2024.
19. Anthony Deutsch, "Reuters photographer Mohammed Salem wins 2024 World Press Photo of the Year award", Reuters, Amsterdam, 18 April 2024.
20. Rami Abou Jamous, *Journal de bord de Gaza*, Montreuil, Libertalia, 2024.
21. "Gaza, fuir l'enfer", broadcast by BFMTV on 17 November 2023.
22. Madjid Zerrouky and Arthur Carpentier, "À Gaza, la destruction méthodique des infrastructures médiatiques", *Le Monde*, 25 June 2024.
23. "How Hamas uses brutality to maintain power", *The New York Times*, 13 September 2024.
24. Jean-Pierre Filiu, *Je vous écris d'Alep*, Denoël, 2013, pp. 99–103.
25. Amira Hass, *Drinking the Sea at Gaza [trans. Elana Wesley & Maxine Kaufman-Lacusta]*, Henry Holt, 1999.
26. Claire Guillot, "War in Gaza takes center stage at Perpignan photojournalism festival", *Le Monde*, 9 September 2024.
27. "Israel top court rejects foreign media appeal for journalists' access to Gaza", *Times of Israel*, 9 January 2024.
28. Jean-Pierre Filiu, "Le destin de l'Europe en 2024 se jouera à Gaza", *Le Monde,* 31 December 2023.
29. Nick Ut, "A single photo can change the world", *Washington Post*, 2 June 2022.

NOTES

VULTURES

1. See above, p. 38.
2. Statement by Tom Fletcher, Under Secretary General for Humanitarian Affairs and Emergency Relief Coordinator for the UN, New York, 6 January 2025.
3. Document presented to the Security Cabinet of Israel on 22 February 2024.
4. Clothilde Mraffko, "Gaza: new accounts of the 'flour massacre'", *Le Monde*, 9 March 2024.
5. "À Gaza, cinq personnes tuées par un largage d'aide humanitaire", *Le Monde*, 8 March 2024.
6. For comparison, the aid brought in by sea on 15 March 2024 was equivalent to only seven food trucks, which could carry around 30 tonnes, while trucks carrying medicines and other supplies could bring in around 20 tonnes.
7. The attack took place on 1 April 2024. Those killed were three humanitarian workers (a US-Canadian citizen, a Pole and an Australian), their three British security guards and their Palestinian driver.
8. Lorenzo Tondo, "Food charity demands independent inquiry into Israeli killing of aid staff", *The Guardian*, 4 April 2024.
9. Statement by Tedros Adhamon Ghebreyesus, WHO Director General, Geneva, 12 June 2024.
10. OCHA, "Reported impact snapshot, Gaza", 31 December 2024.
11. Around thirty-five prisoners have died in detention (Office of the UN High Commissioner for Human Rights, "Detention in the context of the escalation of hostilities in Gaza", 31 July 2024, p. 14).
12. "Gangs looting Gaza aid operate in areas under Israeli control, aid groups say", *Washington Post*, 18 November 2024.
13. "Looting cripples food supply in Gaza as Israel neglects pledge to tackle gangs, sources say", Reuters, Jerusalem, 24 December 2024.
14. Jason Burke, "Aid officials recount violent looting in Gaza as criminal gangs thrive amid Israeli bombardment", *The Guardian*, 29 November 2024.

NOTES

15. Jason Burke, "Gaza ministry says 20 killed in anti-'gang' operation after looting of aid convoy", *The Guardian*, 18 November 2024.
16. To use the medical nomenclature, the BBO (Beaten By Others) briefly outnumbered other kinds of NAT (Non-Accidental Trauma).
17. Emmanuel Fabian, "Katz orders IDF plan for 'complete defeat of Hamas' if no hostage deal by Jan. 20", *Times of Israel*, 10 January 2024.
18. Statement by Tom Fletcher, Under Secretary General for Humanitarian Affairs and Emergency Relief Coordinator for the UN, New York, 6 January 2025.

DEATH

1. Alessandra Bajec, "An open-air graveyard", *New Arab*, 3 January 2024.
2. David Gritten, "Mass grave reports at Gaza hospitals", BBC, 24 April 2024.
3. "At least 16 cemeteries in Gaza desecrated by Israeli forces", CNN, 20 January 2024.
4. OCHA, "Reported impact snapshot, Gaza", 31 December 2024.
5. UNRWA, "Education under attack", 9 September 2024.
6. UNICEF, "Gaza's children are seeing their schools destroyed", 21 November 2024.
7. UNICEF press release, 14 July 2024.
8. Karen McVeigh, "We can't give up on 1 million children", *The Guardian*, 8 December 2024.
9. Statement by Philippe Lazzarini, UNRWA Commissioner General, 12 March 2024.
10. Madjid Zerrouky, "Gaza's Health Ministry reveals names of several thousand dead, over 11,355 of them are minors", *Le Monde*, 21 September 2024.
11. "Traumatic injury mortality in the Gaza Strip from Oct. 7, 2023, to June 30, 2024: a capture–recapture analysis", *The Lancet*, 9 January 2025.
12. UN Women press release, 16 April 2024.
13. "'Orphanage city' in Gaza", UN News, 4 October 2024.

NOTES

14. Laure Stephan, "Gazan orphans face suffering beyond territory's borders", *Le Monde*, 4 July 2024.
15. The scale of the problem is so great that the international organisations refer to it by the acronym WCNSF (wounded child no surviving family).
16. Joint press release by UNRWA, WHO, UNICEF and UNFPA, 3 November 2023.
17. "Pregnant women at risk as Israel cuts off humanitarian aid", *Euronews*, 20 November 2024.
18. OCHA, "Humanitarian situation update 220, Gaza", 20 September 2024.
19. UNFPA, "Palestine situation report", 22 May 2024.
20. Ruwaida Amer, "'Broken': Domestic violence impacts women, children in Gaza", Al-Jazeera, 25 December 2024.
21. AFP, "More war debris in Gaza than Ukraine: UN", 1 May 2024.
22. Andrew G. Clemmensen, "Explosive remnants: Gaza's literal ticking bomb", Washington Institute for Near East Policy, 12 August 2024.

INGENUITY

1. Weekly situation report of the UN Department of Safety and Security, Gaza, 10 January 2025.
2. Instagram @gazasoupkitchen
3. "Israel says it facilitated transfer of fuel, food, water and medications to Gaza hospitals", *Times of Israel*, 9 January 2025.
4. MSF press release, 8 January 2025.
5. At the start of 2025, there were 3.7 shekels to the euro and 3.6 to the dollar.
6. Sara Roy, *The Gaza Strip: the Political Economy of De-development*, Washington, Institute of Palestine Studies, 1995.
7. World Food Programme, "Market monitor—Gaza", August 2024.
8. Rami Abou Jamous, "Cette pénurie a provoqué l'apparition de nouveaux métiers", *Orient* XXI, 12 August 2024.
9. Mohamed Solaimane, "Makeshift mud homes become a fragile winter refuge for displaced Palestinians in southern Gaza", *The New Arab*, 14 January 2025.

NOTES

10. Porter Anderson, "Gaza bookseller Samir Mansour wins the 2024 IPA Prix Voltaire", *Publishing Perspectives*, 5 December 2024.
11. Nagham Mohanna, "Palestinian author on verge of selling book collection to feed Gazans", *The National*, 21 November 2024.

SMOKE

1. Jean-Pierre Filiu, *Stupéfiant Moyen-Orient*, Paris, Le Seuil, 2023, pp. 44–46.
2. Rami Abou Jamous, "Les Israéliens utilisent une nouvelle arme, celle de la cigarette", *Orient XXI*, 29 April 2024.
3. Nabih Bulos and Laura King, "$32 for one cigarette? In Gaza, even a nicotine fix is hard to come by", *Los Angeles Times*, 2 July 2024.
4. "At $25 each, cigarettes are turning Gaza aid trucks into targets", *Wall Street Journal*, 19 June 2024.
5. "Smoking is bad, but Hamas is worse: IDF airdrops cigarettes over Khan Yunis, Gaza", *Jerusalem Post*, 9 August 2024.

WAITING

1. World Food Programme press release, 6 January 2025.
2. Amir Tibon, "Trump vows to 'unleash hell' if Hamas doesn't release the hostages", *Haaretz*, 9 January 2025.
3. Jake Sullivan, *Israel National News*, 12 January 2025.
4. These figures come from the daily summary of hostilities published by the Israeli daily newspaper *Haaretz*.
5. Omar Shaban, "Imagine what the Gaza [sic] will be doing first", Palthink, 15 January 2025.
6. Statement by Sheikh Mohammed Ben Abderrahmane Al Thani, Doha, 15 January 2025.
7. IFHR press release, 17 January 2025.
8. Shabat was killed on 24 March 2025 in a strike claimed by Israel.
9. Jean-Pierre Filiu, "The Gaza ceasefire deal: A house of cards", *Le Monde*, 19 January 2025.
10. Jean-Pierre Filiu, "The death of Holocaust historian Alex Dancyg in captivity in Gaza", *Le Monde*, 29 July 2024.
11. Mohammed Sinwar was killed in Khan Younis by an Israeli airstrike on 13 May 2025.

12. Maram Humaid, "'My children, my children': The Gaza family killed minutes before ceasefire", Al Jazeera, 19 January 2025.

TRUCE

1. Fergal Keane, "'I want to fulfil my dead brother's dream'—rebuilding life in Gaza's ruins", BBC, 20 January 2025.
2. Todd Prince, "Trump again vows to end Ukraine war, warns Taliban about weapons", RFERL, 20 January 2025.
3. "Trump says he's 'not confident' Gaza ceasefire will hold", CNN, 21 January 2025.
4. Stendhal, *Lucien Leuwen*, Paris, Folio, 2002, p. 391.

ONE-FIFTH

1. Benedict Garman and Richard Irvine-Brown, "Gaza 'humanitarian zone' struck almost 100 times since May, BBC Verify finds", BBC, 15 January 2025.
2. Clothilde Mraffko, "In Gaza, thousands of sick and wounded risk dying due to lack of medical evacuations", *Le Monde*, 21 December 2024.

SAMSON

1. Piotr Smolar, "La bande de Gaza au bord de l'asphyxie", *Le Monde*, 20 February 2018.
2. Israeli defence ministry press release, Tel Aviv, 17 February 2025.
3. Yuval Noah Harari, "From Gaza to Iran, the Netanyahu government is endangering Israel's survival", *Haaretz*, 18 April 2024.
4. Andrey Kurkov, *The Silver Bone*, translated by Boris Dralyuk, London, MacLehose Press, 2024, p. 97.